# Introduction to Reparation for Secondary Schools

# INTRODUCTION TO
# REPARATION
## FOR SECONDARY SCHOOLS

Verene A. Shepherd

and

Gabrielle D.L. Hemmings

The University of the West Indies Press
Jamaica • Barbados • Trinidad and Tobago

The Centre for Reparation Research
The University of the West Indies

*in collaboration with*

The CARICOM Reparations Commission

The University of the West Indies Press
7A Gibraltar Hall Road, Mona
Kingston 7, Jamaica
www.uwipress.com

The Centre for Reparation Research
The University of the West Indies

The CARICOM Reparations Commission

© 2022 by The Caribbean Community (CARICOM) Secretariat

All rights reserved. Published 2022

A catalogue record of this book is available from the
National Library of Jamaica.

ISBN: 978-976-640-866-4 (print)
978-976-640-868-8 (ePub)

*Cover image*: Monument to Chief Cuffy (Kofi), leader of the 1763 Berbice War. Used with the kind permission of the Guyana National Trust, Georgetown, Guyana.

Set in Minion Pro 11/14 x 24
Cover and book design by Robert Harris

The University of the West Indies Press has no responsibility for the persistence or accuracy of URLs for external or third-party Internet websites referred to in this publication and does not guarantee that any content on such websites is, or will remain, accurate or appropriate.

Printed in the United States of America

# Contents

List of Figures / *vi*

List of Tables / *vii*

Preface and Acknowledgements / *ix*

Abbreviations / *xii*

Introduction / *1*

1. Reparatory Justice: Regional and Global Contexts / *6*
2. Justification for Reparation / *16*
3. Setting Out the Caribbean Case for Reparation / *47*
4. The Strategy: The CARICOM Ten-Point Plan / *63*
5. No Apology, No Reparation: Europe's Stance / *73*
6. Small Steps, Giant Leaps for Reparation / *87*

**Appendix:** Select Compensation Claims for the Caribbean (Male), Ranked from Highest to Lowest, Showing Modern-Day Equivalencies / *101*

Selected Bibliography / *103*

# Figures

2.1. Statue of Christopher Columbus, St Ann's Bay, Jamaica / **17**

2.2. Monument to Joseph Chatoyer (Satuye), Garifuna warrior from St Vincent and the Grenadines / **19**

2.3. The *Zong* monument, Black River, Jamaica / **22**

5.1. Clovis commentary on the *Zong* massacre and reparation / **85**

# Tables

2.1. Summary of European participation in the transatlantic trade in Africans, 1526–1864   /   **44**

2.2. Extract of slavers that trafficked enslaved Africans to the Caribbean   /   **45**

3.1. A sample of reparation settlements   /   **59**

# Preface and Acknowledgements

The Caribbean Examinations Council (CXC) has taken the bold step to include reparation and reconciliation in the Caribbean Advanced Proficiency Examination (CAPE) syllabus. This is in tandem with the Caribbean Secondary Education Certificate (CSEC) syllabus, which, by teaching about precolonial and colonial African societies; the Caribbean preconquest; conquest, colonization, slavery, emancipation and indentureship (especially Indian indentureship); as well as about independence and decolonization, provides the historical justification for the reparatory justice movement. This campaign for reparatory justice is now a global movement which calls on those who colonized the people of the Caribbean and other parts of the world to apologize for their actions and repair the damage caused, especially through genocide against the Indigenous Peoples and the trafficking in, and enslavement of, Africans. The Programme of Activities for the United Nations International Decade for People of African Descent (2015–2024) also calls on states that benefited from what are now increasingly being recognized as crimes against humanity to apologize and engage in reparation, where they have not already done so. CARICOM states have taken this seriously and sent letters about reparation to relevant European states, but there has been no positive response to these letters from such states.

Furthermore, former colonizing nations have not responded to the general demand for reparatory justice in the way demanded by the descendants of historically affected people. However, churches, individuals whose families benefited from slavery, financial institutions and educational institutions, like law schools and universities, have been researching their links to slavery and colonialism and engaging with people of African descent and Indigenous Peoples in a reparatory justice conversation. Most notable are the University of Glasgow and Harvard Law School. The University of Cambridge in the United Kingdom has also begun a process of researching its links to slavery and considering its reparatory justice obligations. One of its colleges, Jesus, has independently established the Legacy of Slavery Working Party to study that college's benefits from slavery and colonialism. Some churches have even apologized.

This booklet will help secondary school students, in particular CAPE-level history students, to understand the meaning of reparation, the reasons Caribbean governments and people believe it is a just cause, the long history of the movement, the objectives of the movement, and the forms that reparation should take, including repatriation to Africa for those who desire it. Above all, students will be introduced to the idea that reparation is a right, not an act of begging. Reparation has the potential to achieve peace and reconciliation between the descendants of the former colonizers and the descendants of the victims. South Africa saw the benefits of reconciliation, which is why, post-apartheid, it established the Truth and Reconciliation Commission, which is also discussed in this volume.

The production of this booklet would not have been possible without the contribution of several individuals and entities, among them Ian Randle, who wrote the first draft with the assistance of the Centre for Reparation research; Clovis Brown and the Guyana National Trust, who graciously permitted the use of their images; the CARICOM Reparations Commission and the staff of the Centre for Reparation Research. Finally, we thank the late Dr Joseph Powell, who was general manager of the University of the West Indies Press when the agreement was reached to publish this resource booklet, and other members of the University of the West Indies Press team (not least the keen-eyed Shivaun Hearne) for finalizing the project, which was dear to Joe's heart.

As you use this booklet to help you pass your history examinations, we salute you for studying history, a dying discipline in the

Caribbean, regrettably. You understand Marcus Garvey's cautionary words well: "A people without the knowledge of their past history, origin and culture is like a tree without roots." The Sankofa adinkra symbol used throughout this text is another way of representing this thought – going back to roots to understand the present.

# Abbreviations

| | |
|---|---|
| CARICOM | Caribbean Community |
| CRC | CARICOM Reparations Commission |
| TRC | Truth and Reconciliation Commission |
| TTA | transatlantic trade in enslaved Africans |

# Introduction

The inclusion of reparation in schools' curricula as an essential part of Caribbean history is long overdue. From a historical perspective, reparation should be viewed as the final act in the over-five-hundred-year struggle that began with the fight against conquest and colonization, the trade in Indigenous Peoples and Africans, African enslavement, and deceptive indentureship and ended with the achievement of independence and self-determination in the mid-twentieth century for some Caribbean countries. In this twenty-first century, the fight for reparatory justice continues for the Indigenous People who were descendants of the victims of genocide; the descendants of the victims of the transatlantic trade in enslaved Africans (TTA), chattel enslavement and deceptive Asian indentureship.

No study of Caribbean history can be complete without an examination and appreciation of this ongoing struggle that represents the final link required to close the circle which began with two of the worst crimes in human history: Indigenous Peoples' genocide and African chattel enslavement. The struggle must end with atonement and restitution by the perpetrators, on the one hand, and redemption for the descendants of the victims, on the other. Without atonement, restitution and redemption, there can be no true peace. As reggae singer Peter Tosh declared, "Everyone is crying out for peace, no one is crying out for justice. . . . I need equal rights and justice."[1]

Before we embark on a study of reparation in the Caribbean context, it is important to point out that it is not an act that can be isolated to a particular country or place or frozen in time. Rather, it is a *movement* and a *process* that is at times tangible and at other

---

1. Peter Tosh, "Equal Rights", track 5 on *Equal Rights* (Rolling Stone, 1977).

times intangible. Just as we would not say today that emancipation from chattel slavery began in 1807 with the supposed ending of the TTA to the British-colonized Caribbean, or in 1838 with the final ending of slavery in the British-colonized Caribbean, so we would not say that reparation struggles began recently. In fact, we must interpret the resistant activities of Indigenous Peoples and enslaved Africans and later of indentured Asians as acts seeking redress for wrongs. We look, therefore, at the spirit and acts of individuals like Sally Bassett of Bermuda, Queen Nanny (or Nana) of the Jamaican Maroons, Chief Tacky (Takyi), Ann James, Samuel Sharpe and Paul Bogle of Jamaica, Alida of Suriname, King Cuffy (Kofi), Nanny Grigg and Bussa of Barbados, King Satuye of St Vincent and the Grenadines, and King Court of Antigua and Barbuda, among others. They were among the early activists. Since then, the movement has expanded through increased advocacy by the Rastafari, civil society organizations, individual politicians, scholar-activists and now governments of the Caribbean Community (CARICOM) as a bloc. Therefore, what began as a dream by African ancestors and post-slavery and modern activists (for example, Rastafari and those who gathered at the First Pan African Congress on Reparations in 1993 in Abuja, Nigeria) has gained formal recognition and establishment through the National Council on Reparation (formerly the Jamaica National Commission on Reparations, established 2009), the CARICOM Reparations Commission (CRC, established 2013), and several national committees across the Caribbean, the Americas, Africa and Europe.

In pursuit of its mandate to educate, enlighten and convert a new generation of Caribbean youth about reparation, the CRC, through the Centre for Reparation Research, sets out in this volume to provide justification for the demand for reparation and a historical overview of what is now the Caribbean reparation movement and its achievements to date.

Chapter 1, "Reparatory Justice: Regional and Global Contexts", begins with an explanation of the concept of reparatory justice and places it concretely in the Caribbean context of the crimes against humanity committed by some Europeans. The Caribbean reparation movement and its origins and historical development are examined in its national, regional and global dimensions. Early global initiatives (including the First Pan African Congress on Reparations, held in Abuja, Nigeria, in 1993, the seminal UN World Conference against Racism, Discrimination, Xenophobia and Related Intolerance held in Durban, South Africa, in 2001, and Haiti's just claim on France for reparations in 2004) are highlighted as watersheds in the movement in which the Caribbean was an important player and influencer. Special mention is made of the historic decision by the Jamaican Parliament to establish the National Commission on Reparations in 2009 and the decision made by the CARICOM Heads of Government to establish the CRC in 2013, signalling a regional demand for reparation.

Chapter 2, "Justification for Reparation", is in two parts. Part 1 focuses on the double crime perpetrated by named European countries against Indigenous Peoples and Africans and, later on, against those subjected to various forms of contractual unfreedoms. Students are exposed to the most current research findings of the Slave Voyages Database 2.0 (2018), which helps to identify a new list of perpetrators, adding to the known illegal human traffickers and the dates and numbers of Africans they loaded, transported and offloaded over some 36,000 voyages. Data collected and analysed by the Centre for the Study of the Legacies of British Slave-Ownership (now the Centre for the Study of the Legacies of British Slavery) at University College London are introduced and used to identify state, institutional and individual *beneficiaries* of African enslavement to whom claims for reparation should be made. It should be noted that it was Tufts University professor Kris Manjapra who alerted us in the Caribbean to startling new information on the financial institutions that loaned the British government the £20 million that was paid to enslavers at Emancipation as compensation, loans that were not paid off in their entirety until 2015.

Part 2 of chapter 2 goes beyond naming the usual suspects to include those European countries that were neither colonial powers nor the operators of large-scale plantation systems employing enslaved labour in the Caribbean. However, they are equally implicated as illicit traders in enslaved Africans, operators of ports and forts in West Africa, suppliers of labour and goods to slavers and enslavers, as well as manufacturers and suppliers of equipment of navigation, torture and production. Each case against Spain, the United Kingdom, Portugal, France, the Netherlands, Denmark, Sweden, Norway, Germany, and Switzerland is laid out individually.

Chapter 3, "Setting Out the Caribbean Case for Reparation", examines the legal, economic, moral and other bases on which the demand for reparation is made. It draws heavily on the works of reparation scholar-activists Hilary Beckles, Dudley Thompson and Anthony Gifford. The bases for what constitutes a meritorious claim are discussed and convincingly established, in the process citing numerous precedents for the admission of guilt, expression of apologies and the payment of financial compensation by countries including Germany, the United Kingdom and the United States.

Chapter 4, "The Strategy: The CARICOM Ten-Point Plan", examines the agreed CARICOM Ten-Point Plan for Reparatory Justice, with its detailed outline of the rationale and basis for each of the ten demands.

Chapter 5, "No Apology, No Reparation: Europe's Stance", examines the responses by various European nations and total denial by the British in particular even to engage in discussion on the subject. Arguments are presented to counteract the claim by apologists that slavery was legal at the time and that Africa should shoulder the major responsibility for the TTA. An important distinction is made between expressing "regret" and issuing a full and formal "apology".

Chapter 6, "Small Steps, Giant Leaps for Reparation", covers the period from 2013, when CARICOM threw its support behind the reparation movement, to the present, detailing small but important advances in the progress of the movement, particularly at the level of universities, corporations and financial institutions. Equally significant are developments in the United States, where the issue of reparation was placed at the forefront of the #BlackLivesMatter movement (a movement that has now become globalized following the murder of African American George Floyd) and on the agenda of the 2020 presidential election campaign, which was won by Joe Biden, with Kamala Harris as the first African American woman to be elected vice president. The chapter also considers the potential of reparation settlements to bring peace and reconciliation to the world. The text concludes with a selected bibliography of the key books and articles as well as online resources that students will find useful.

In your readings on the topic, you will have seen the words *reparation* and *reparations* variously used. While *reparations* means forms of compensation provided, including monetary payments, the authors' preference is to use *reparation*, which is the act or process of making amends for wrongdoing, including financial compensation. Note well, too, the ways in which the text attempts to decolonize the language used throughout in order to be more respectful of the experiences of Caribbean people and avoid the use of certain words like *slave, slaves, slave trade, masters/mistresses*, and so on. We prefer *enslaved men/women/people*, which puts the blame on the colonizers for chattel enslavement; and *enslavers* more accurately describes those who enslaved African ancestors. The *transatlantic trade in enslaved Africans* should replace *slave trade*. Please ensure that you make the use of the new terms a part of your own vocabulary.

# 1

# Reparatory Justice
## Regional and Global Contexts

The concept of reparatory justice emphasizes repairing the harm caused the criminal action of an individual, group or nation against another. When we speak of reparation, it is meant to describe the act of redressing or repairing wrongs that have been done and to remove the long-term effects of the crimes and wrongs upon the victims and their descendants. In international law, it is a recognized principle that nations or individuals who have wronged other nations or individuals should make reparation or repair the damage. When applied in the Caribbean context, the crimes and wrongs to which we refer are the genocide of Indigenous Peoples, the illegal and inhuman transatlantic trade in enslaved Africans, African chattel enslavement, and the criminal institution of slavery that lasted for centuries. The call for reparatory justice is also applied to the terrible aspects of Asian indentureship (introduced to the British-colonized Caribbean and Suriname by the British) and the legacies of colonialism in the Caribbean. It identifies the *perpetrators* of these crimes and wrongs as named countries of Europe and the *victims* as Indigenous Peoples, enslaved Africans, indentured labourers and their descendants, where they continue to suffer harm. Reparatory justice seeks an unequivocal acknowledgement by the guilty nations of Europe that wrong was done and for them to make amends through monetary compensation, repatriation of looted artefacts and displaced people, infrastructural development, technology transfer and debt cancellation.

In 2013, the CARICOM Heads of Government formalized the longstanding movement for reparatory justice in the Caribbean with the establishment of the CRC. They also mandated the formation of national committees for reparation in member states where there were none. We describe the movement as "longstanding" because way before 2013, Indigenous Peoples struggled against conquest and colonization and insisted on their human rights. The Indigenous Peoples' wars of resistance included the Spanish and Taino War of San Juan-Borikén in Puerto Rico (1511), the Taino War led by Hatuey in Cuba (1511–1512), the Taino War led by Enriquillo in Hispaniola (1519) and the First Garifuna War in St Vincent (1769–1773). The atrocities committed against the Indigenous Peoples form part of the justification for insisting on reparatory justice.

Enslaved Africans opposed chattel slavery. In his path-breaking book *Britain's Black Debt: Reparations for Caribbean Slavery and Native Genocide*,[2] historian Hilary Beckles writes that the pioneers of the reparation movement for Africans were the enslaved Africans who knew their illegal capture and forced relocation to the Americas were a violation of their human rights and struggled to end the Maangamizi (African holocaust). The enslaved-led wars all over the Caribbean, including the seventeenth-century Maroon Wars in Jamaica which ended in treaty arrangements, represented a search for reparatory justice through freedom. The 1757 Tempati War in Surinam (now Suriname); the 1760, 1824 and 1831–1832 wars in Jamaica; the 1763 (Berbice) and 1823 (Demerara) wars in British Guiana (now Guyana); the Haitian Revolution (1791–1804); the 1816 War in Barbados; and La Escalera in Cuba (1843–1844) are prime examples of resistance. Of all the above, the Haitian Revolution was the first to lead to emancipation and independence. Then, in the post-slavery period, the newly emancipated in all of the Americas

---

2. Hilary McD. Beckles, *Britain's Black Debt: Reparations for Caribbean Slavery and Native Genocide* (Kingston: University of the West Indies Press, 2013).

continued the struggle, protesting the attempts of colonizers to continue the relations of production of the previous era. Indentured and post-indentured Indians protested their treatment by plantation owners and the non-implementation of contractual terms. In the 1920s and 1930s, Marcus Garvey emerged to speak of reparation for the crimes committed against Africans,[3] and in the 1930s, the labour protests and the franchise and independence movements all continued the search for reparatory justice. Finally, the post-1930s advocates for reparatory justice were the Rastafari, whose claim was for African redemption and repatriation. Prior to the CARICOM mandate establishing national commissions, Jamaica had taken a decisive step in this direction in 2009: for the first time in the history of the British-colonized Caribbean, a sitting government appointed a national commission on reparation, chaired by the late Barry Chevannes. This 2009 initiative by the Government of Jamaica was driven by member of Parliament Lester Michael "Mike" Henry, a lifelong advocate for reparation in Jamaica, and supported by member of Parliament Olivia "Babsy" Grange, who had (and, up to the time of publication, still has) portfolio responsibility for reparation.

### Reparation: The Global Dimension

The Caribbean is only a part of the international movement for reparatory justice. In the international realm, global initiatives such as the Durban Declaration and Programme of Action, born out of the 2001 United Nations World Conference against Racism and the International Decade for People of African Descent, have helped to strengthen the resolve to continue the reparatory justice fight. The Durban Declaration acknowledges that "historical injustices have undeniably contributed to the poverty, underdevelopment, marginalization, social exclusion, economic disparities, instability and insecurity that affect many people in different parts of the world,

---

3. IBI21, "Marcus Garvey on Reparations", Institute of the Black World 21st Century, 4 August 2017, https://ibw21.org/reparations/marcus-garvey-reparations/.

in particular in developing countries".[4] With this recognition that the present disparities experienced by people of African descent are due to a history of enslavement and colonialism, the argument for reparation, globally, is further justified.

The International Decade for People of African Descent, proclaimed as such by the UN General Assembly for the period 2015–2024, has aided in strengthening the resolve for the need for reparatory justice through its explicit reference to reparation. Under the Programme of Activities, influenced by the Durban Declaration and Programme of Action, we find its dedication to the tenet of justice:

> acknowledging and profoundly regretting the untold suffering and evils inflicted on millions of men, women and children as a result of slavery, the slave trade, the transatlantic slave trade, colonialism, apartheid, genocide and past tragedies, noting that some States have taken the initiative to apologize and have paid reparation, where appropriate, for grave and massive violations committed, and calling on those that have not yet expressed remorse or presented apologies to find some way to contribute to the restoration of the dignity of victims.[5]

This explicit reference has further strengthened the resolve for reparation for people of African descent globally.

Internationally, the reparation movement has come a long way and homage must be paid to the contributions of the 1993 First Pan African Conference on Reparations and the 2001 UN-organized Conference against Racism, Racial Discrimination, Xenophobia and Related Intolerance in Durban, South Africa. However, while these two conferences are often cited as monumental in the global reparation movement, in tracing the genealogy of the movement in

---

4. "Declaration of the World Conference against Racism, Racial Discrimination, Xenophobia and Related Intolerance", https://www.un.org/en/durbanreview2009/pdf/DDPA_full_text.pdf.

5. United Nations, "Resolution Adopted by the General Assembly on 18 November 2014", A/RES/69/16, 1 December 2014, https://www.un.org/en/observances/decade-people-african-descent/justice.

its international dimension, recognition of pre-1993 activism must be made. In fact, in the United States, the Commission to Study and Develop Reparation Proposals for African-Americans Act (popularly known as HR 40) was first introduced in the US Congress from as early as 1989 by Democratic congressman John Conyers Jr. Until 2021, it had been reintroduced every year since then, with limited success until recently (see chapter 6). But it helped set the stage for the First Pan African Conference on Reparations in 1993.

## The Abuja Proclamation

The Abuja Conference was held in Abuja, Nigeria, from 27 to 29 April 1993. It was chaired by Chief Moshood Abiola, and attended by hundreds of representatives from thirty countries, including Abdou Diouf, then chairman of the Organization of African Unity (now the African Union), Tanzanian secretary general of the then Organization of African Unity Salim Ahmed Salim, and Jamaican human rights lawyer and diplomat Ambassador Dudley Thompson, who served as rapporteur. Thompson encapsulated the position of the conference by stating that reparation was "not a plea for charity".[6] It was also here that British/Jamaican advocate Lord Anthony Gifford, by invitation of Thompson, summarized the legal justification for reparation, as follows:

1. The enslavement of Africans was a crime against humanity.
2. International law recognizes that those who commit crimes against humanity must make reparation.
3. The reparation claim would be brought on behalf of all Africans, in Africa and the diaspora, who suffer the consequences of the crime, through the agency of an appropriate representative.
4. There is no legal barrier to prevent those who suffer the consequences of crimes against humanity from claiming reparation, even though the crimes were committed against their ancestors.
5. The claim would be brought against the governments of those

---

6. Beckles, *Britain's Black Debt*, 178.

countries which promoted and were enriched by the TTA and the institution of slavery.
6. The claim, if not settled by agreement, would be determined by a special international tribunal recognized by all parties.[7]

At the end of the conference, the representatives issued the Abuja Proclamation,[8] which

- declared that the damage sustained by African peoples was not a "thing of the past" but is painfully manifested in the damaged lives of contemporary Africans everywhere;
- urged those countries that were enriched by slavery to give total relief from foreign debt;
- emphasized that what matters is not the guilt but the responsibility of those states and nations whose economic evolution depended on enslaved labourers and colonialism; and
- recommended the establishment of national reparation commissions in Africa and the diaspora.

The ending of apartheid in South Africa and ascendancy to leadership of Nelson Mandela and the African National Congress in May 1994 provided a unique opportunity for the concept of reparatory justice to be practically applied to achieve healing and reconciliation.

## South Africa's Truth and Reconciliation Commission

In the case of South Africa, a new dimension was added to the idea of reparatory justice in the concept of *restorative* justice, which was the bedrock of the Truth and Reconciliation Commission (TRC) that was set up by the Government of the Republic of South Africa in 1995, in the aftermath of the end of apartheid. Restorative justice

---

7. Beckles, *Britain's Black Debt*, 177–78. See also Anthony Gifford, "The Legal Basis of the Claim for Slavery Reparation", *Human Rights Magazine* 27, 2 (2000), https://www.americanbar.org/groups/crsj/publications/human_rights_magazine_home/human_rights_vol27_2000/spring2000/hr_spring00_gifford/.

8. "The Abuja Proclamation", http://ncobra.org/resources/pdf/TheAbujaProclamation.pdf.

is an approach in which the response to a crime (apartheid) is to bring the victim and the offender together to share the experience of what happened, to discuss who was harmed and how, and to arrive at a consensus on what the offender can do to repair the harm of the offence. This may include formal apologies and other actions to compensate those affected. The mandate of the TRC was to bear witness to, record and, in some cases, grant amnesty to the perpetrators of crimes relating to human rights violations, as well as offer reparation and rehabilitation to the victims. An important feature of the TRC deliberations was its emphasis on restorative justice, with the aim being *reconciliation* as opposed to *retributive* justice involving punishment.

The report of the TRC published in 1998 included testimonies from 22,000 victims and witnesses.[9] Among other things, the TRC recommended compensation for victims, and criminal charges to be laid against alleged perpetrators. While it is generally acknowledged that the TRC was a necessary and useful exercise, critics hold the view that it failed to achieve reconciliation between the black and white communities and that it was weighted in favour of the perpetrators of abuse. As proof of the alleged bias, they point to the fact that no case recommended for prosecution was brought before the courts and that, overall, most of the recommendations of the TRC have not been implemented. Moreover, the state has not formally instituted any reparation programmes, and actions, such as they are, have been largely symbolic, in the form of freedom parks, museums, and the naming and renaming of public places.

## The Conference against Racism, Racial Discrimination, Xenophobia and Related Intolerance

The 2001 UN-organized Conference against Racism, Racial Discrimination, Xenophobia and Related Intolerance in Durban, South

---

9. TRC, *Truth and Reconciliation Commission of South Africa Report*, 7 vols. (Pretoria: Department of Justice and Constitutional Development), https://www.justice.gov.za/trc/report/.

Africa, attempted, in the words of Barbados's representative Hilary Beckles, to move the discourse "from rhetoric to action". It was a historic forum that saw gathered, for the first time, heads of state and nongovernmental organizations discussing face to face the subject of Europe's historical crimes and injustice.

The official position of the Caribbean governments was that a global reparation agenda should be established and that there should be a meaningful dialogue about repairing the damage caused by slavery and colonization within the context of international law. While Caribbean advocates might have taken some comfort in resolutions that were adopted condemning the trading in enchained and enslaved Africans and declaring the TTA and slavery "crimes against humanity", these were non-binding on countries that have been criminally enriched by these activities. Beyond that, European nations present showed no willingness to discuss reparation. At the heart of their strategy was avoidance and refusal to accept the validity of historical data. They insisted that slavery and the TTA were not crimes against humanity when they were committed and, in the case of the British, argued that national and colonial laws ensured their legality:

> We acknowledge that slavery and the slave trade, including the transatlantic slave trade, were appalling tragedies in the history of humanity not only because of their abhorrent barbarism but also in terms of their magnitude, organized nature and especially their negation of the essence of the victims, and further acknowledge that slavery and the slave trade are a crime against humanity and should always have been so, especially the transatlantic slave trade, and are among the major sources and manifestations of racism, racial discrimination, xenophobia and related intolerance, and that Africans and people of African descent, Asians and people of Asian descent and indigenous peoples were victims of these acts and continue to be victims of their consequences.[10]

---

10. World Conference against Racism, Racial Discrimination, Xenophobia and Related Intolerance, "Declaration", https://www.un.org/en/durbanreview2009/pdf/DDPA_full_text.pdf; emphasis added.

Caribbean advocates did not endorse this declaration because it failed to recognize slavery and the transatlantic trade as crimes against humanity at the time they were practised. While the Durban Conference was seen as a setback for the reparation movement, the intransigence of the European nations, backed by the United States, only served to strengthen the resolve of Caribbean advocates to bring the guilty nations to the discussion table. There was a decisive change in their strategic thinking and approach. This new approach had three main elements:

1. Intensification of the research and data-gathering to provide incontrovertible evidence of European culpability and brutality in the illegal conduct of the TTA and African enslavement;
2. Presentation of evidence and data gathered in different forums – conferences and so on – to create greater public awareness and gain international support; and
3. Promotion of an active reparation movement in the Caribbean with the endorsement of both national governments and CARICOM.

Added to this controversy was the withdrawal of both Israel and the United States from the conference for varying reasons. On the subject of the United States and the notion of reparation, US representative Colin Powell (then secretary of state), withdrew from attending. One of the key reasons for his withdrawal was the subject of reparation, which the US government argued was not for the United Nations to settle.

One other important trigger should be noted. In 2004, as the bicentenary of Haitian independence approached, that country's president, Jean-Bertrand Aristide, made a formal request to France for the restitution of US$21 billion. This amount was equivalent to the 90 million gold francs it forcibly extracted from Haiti (this was a reduction in the initial French demand for 150 million gold francs) as compensation for the loss of its "property" when Haiti fought and defeated France to gain its independence in 1804. French reaction to the loss of Haiti was to isolate the new nation politically and financially. With the aid of the United States, Britain and Spain, it effectively cut off trade with Haiti, thus stifling the country. On top of that, there were frequent threats of military invasion and re-enslavement of Haitians if they did not pay compensation to France. Faced with a collapsed economy and the threat of the French reconquering Haiti through military invasion, the Haitian government finally capitulated to the French demand in 1825 and began paying compensation to France in yearly instalments. The last instalment was paid in 1947. Aristide's demand in 2004 met with a similar reaction from France and its allies to that of two hundred years earlier, resulting in his arrest and exile (to the Central African Republic, Jamaica and South Africa), the invasion of Haiti by the Americans, the installation of a puppet government, and the official withdrawal of the reparation request by the new government led by Gérard Latortue.[11] Strictly speaking, however, it was not a request for reparation for slavery as a crime against humanity, but a demand for public funds extracted by criminal means by one state from another.

---

11. Hilary Beckles, "The Hate and the Quake: Part II", *Pambazuka News*, 17 March 2010, https://www.pambazuka.org/governance/hate-and-quake-part-ii.

# 2

# Justification for Reparation

Indigenous genocide, the TTA, the system of chattel enslavement and deceptive Asian indentureship in the Caribbean form the major justification for the reparation movement in the Caribbean.

## Indigenous Genocide

Why do historians speak in terms of indigenous genocide?

On 12 October 1492, Italian navigator and explorer Christopher Columbus and his crew, acting with the support of the Spanish monarchy, arrived along the coast of Guanahani (now San Salvador), one of the islands of the archipelago of the Bahamas. Spain, an experienced colonial nation (by virtue of its capture of the Canary Islands), gave support to Columbus, an experienced navigator, who deduced that one could arrive in the East (Asia) by sailing westwards. This support from Spanish monarchs Queen Isabella and King Ferdinand came after failed attempts to convince the Portuguese, French and English to back his quest.

Columbus and his crew had sought to journey to Asia, and upon their arrival in the Caribbean, they believed they were on the outskirts of the Asian continent. When they landed in Guanahani, they encountered the indigenous Tainos, who would be subjected to a force of terror that would lead to their almost complete annihilation.

**Figure 2.1.** Statue of Christopher Columbus in St Ann's Bay, Jamaica

Upon their first brief encounter in Guanahani, Columbus wrote that the Tainos "ought to make good servants".[12] A few days later, Columbus journeyed to Cuba. He and his crew then surveyed the northern region of the Caribbean before departing for Spain and left the crew of his shipwrecked *Santa María* in Hispaniola (now the Dominican Republic and Haiti) to build a fort. On this first

---

12. Hilary McD. Beckles, and Verene A. Shepherd, *Liberties Lost: The Indigenous Caribbean and Slave Systems* (Cambridge: Cambridge University Press, 2004), 37.

voyage, Columbus sailed with three ships. On his second voyage, still believing the Caribbean to be close to the Asian mainland, Columbus, under royal sponsorship, arrived with an increased fleet of seventeen ships in 1494. This time, his expanded fleet explored the eastern Caribbean – prominent Kalinago territory. It was on this voyage that the terror of colonization of the Indigenous Peoples of the region began, starting with Santo Domingo (part of what they called Hispaniola) for the first ten years and then expanding to Cuba, Puerto Rico and Jamaica thereafter.

During their colonial rule, the Spanish almost completely decimated the Indigenous Peoples of the region. Under Columbus (governor and viceroy of the Indies), the Indigenous Peoples were subjected to cruelty and tyranny. The Tainos were forced to obtain food for Spanish settlements and mine for gold in order to pay tribute to the Spanish crown – to the detriment of the Taino economy. During the period from 1498 to 1509, the Spanish implemented the *repartimiento* system, which was later modified to become the *encomienda* system. This system saw the Indigenous Peoples being "shared out" among the Spanish settlers as enslaved labourers and taxpayers. Brutality, torture and exposure to foreign disease led to the demise of the Indigenous Peoples. Historical records portray a chilling picture of the horrifying experiences of Indigenous Peoples under European colonialism. In Hispaniola, for instance, records suggest that while there were approximately 1.2 million "*Indios*" in 1496, by 1514, only around 32,000 Tainos remained. By 1530, only 2,000 remained.[13]

Other European countries would follow suit in their quest for colonial lands. In St Vincent and the Grenadines, for instance, the British colonialism led to the depletion of Kalinago/Garifuna populations. In 1763, there were some 9,000 Kalinago/Garifuna. However, roughly 80 per cent of this population was lost due to diseases brought by the British, starvation and deportation. An estimated 2,500 were killed outright by the British as they sought to

---

13. William F. Keegan and Corinne L. Hofman, *The Caribbean before Columbus* (Oxford: Oxford University Press, 2017), 255; Beckles and Shepherd, *Liberties Lost*, 42.

**Figure 2.2.** Monument to Joseph Chatoyer (Satuye), Garifuna warrior from St Vincent and the Grenadines

fight for their lives and land.[14] It is these numbers that substantiate the argument for reparation for indigenous genocide.

## The Transatlantic Trade in Enslaved Africans

It was Bartolomé de Las Casas who proposed the use of enslaved Africans for labour. An *encomendero* in Cuba, Las Casas argued that if the *encomienda* system remained, the Taino population would be completely wiped out. As a result, he suggested that enslaved Africans be used for labour instead.

The forced transportation of enslaved Africans to the Caribbean and the wider Americas, the permanent dislocation of over 30 million

---

14. "Statement by Dr the Honourable Ralph E. Gonsalves, Prime Minister of St Vincent and the Grenadines, on the Topic of 'Reparations for Slavery and the Genocide of Native Peoples'", OAS, https://www.oas.org/en/media_center/speech.asp?sCodigo=15-0088.

people in communities across the continent of Africa, and the mutilation and murder of millions unknown, constitute modernity's greatest crime against humanity. Estimates of the number of victims of the transatlantic trade conducted over three centuries vary between a low of 12 million and a high of 15 million. But that does not tell the full story: to that figure must be added those who died on the journey and before. Approximately 2 million Africans died during the Atlantic crossing and for every African who left the shores of Africa alive, two to five souls died between the village from which they were captured and the coast. In other words, between 24 and 60 million lost their lives in Africa. The largest number of victims was born during slavery in the Americas. For every African brought alive to the Americas, ten to twelve generations of their offspring were born free and then enslaved directly after birth. If each member of that generation had two to three children, the total number of victims of European slavery would be between 200 and 360 million. When we focus on the British Caribbean, it is estimated that 3.2 million enslaved people were traded by the British, with some 2.6 million disembarking on the shores of their Caribbean colonies between 1662 and 1811. Based on these estimates, the true story of European brutality is to be told by the fact that after three hundred years of trading in black bodies and of African enslavement, there were just about 800,000 enslaved Africans who survived the holocaust of enslavement in the British-colonized Caribbean in 1834. The difference between the numbers traded and the numbers at Emancipation suggests that less than 25 per cent of Africans who were captured and forcibly enslaved survived.

### Chattel Enslavement

The enterprise of capturing and illegally transporting millions of Africans from their homeland to the strange lands of the Americas and facilitating the buying and selling of Africans was itself a crime against humanity. Their enslavement in a system that denied their humanity and violated their human rights, forcing them to work for no pay and brutalizing them, was an even greater crime. Slavery as a system of domination is, of course, an ancient institution, but chattel slavery was a particularly virulent form of evil that had not been practised anywhere in the world before it was introduced into the Caribbean. Chattel slavery defines a subordinate person as property, where the enslaved has no human dignity because property is not human and therefore devoid of dignity. This means the enslaved could be bought and sold, mortgaged, rented and replaced when their value depreciated, used as investments, and brutalized. Chattel slavery was racially defined, attached only to Africans, reproduced through the African female and sanctioned through the legislative acts of various parliaments and British courts.

Chattel slavery was particularly brutal for enslaved African women, who bore the brunt of the enslavers' force. In the fields, they were the backbone of the labour force. They were rarely allowed to preserve family life and they were constantly whipped, imprisoned, raped or executed. In the book *The History of Mary Prince*, Prince recounted that her enslaver "after abusing me with every ill name he could think of, and giving me several hard blows with his hand . . . [said], I shall come home tomorrow morning at twelve, on purpose and give you a round hundred. He kept his word. . . . He tied me up upon a ladder; Benjy stood by to count them for him. When he had licked me for some time he sat down to take breath; then after resting, be beat me again . . . there was a dreadful earthquake . . . during the confusion I crawled away on my hands and knees."[15] The sexual abuse of African women is especially well-documented and reflected in the voices of Thomas Thistlewood, Robert Wedderburn and Orlando Patterson. Patterson graphically depicts the culture of sexual abuse towards women in Jamaica, stating: "The sexual exploitation of female slaves by white men was the most disgraceful aspect of Jamaican slave society. Rape and the seduction of infant slaves, the ravishing of the common-law wives of the male slaves under the threat of punishment, and outright sadism often involving

---

15. Mary Prince, "The History of Mary Prince", in *Caribbean Slavery in the Atlantic World*, ed. Verene A. Shepherd and Hilary McD. Beckles (Kingston: Ian Randle, 2000), 847.

the most heinous forms of sexual torture were the order of the day."[16]

The most outrageous example of the prevailing philosophy that saw Africans as being less than human and more as property is told in the tragedy of the slaver *Zong* in the presentation by Verene Shepherd reproduced here (see text box).[17] A monument now stands to memorialize the 132 victims of the *Zong* massacre in Black River, St Elizabeth, Jamaica (see figure 2.3).

**Figure 2.3.** The *Zong* monument in Black River, Jamaica

---

16. Orlando Patterson, *The Sociology of Slavery: An Analysis of the Origins, Development, and Structure of Negro Slave Society in Jamaica* (London: McGibbon and Kee, 1967), 42.

17. Verene Shepherd, "Before and After the *Zong*: Murder and Racial Discrimination in African Diaspora History" (Ministry of Culture, Gender, Entertainment and Sport and the National Council on Reparation, Jamaica, webinar commemorating the *Zong* massacre, 22 December 2020).

## "Before and after the *Zong*: Murder and Racial Discrimination in African Diaspora History"

I start by singing praise songs to the three African men who arrived on the *Zong* but who ran away four months later. The advertisement in the *Cornwall Chronicle* read:

> Hopewell, Trelawny,
>
> Run away, from the Subscriber around four weeks ago, three new Negro men of the Chamba or Coromantee country; speak no English, having been only four months in the country, but are all marked on the right shoulder IC, D on top. Any person taking up all or either of said Negroes, or sending them to gaol, or the Subscriber at the above Estate, shall receive twenty Shillings for each, and all reasonable charges; but if any person be found to harbour or conceal them, they may depend on being prosecuted as the law directs. JOHN CHRYSTIE.

My knowledge of that act of defiance introduces a modicum of celebration amidst this sorrowful memory of the journey of the *Zong*.

In 1781, a Liverpool merchant syndicate of William, John and James Gregson, Edward Wilson and James Aspinall, on a slaving voyage in the area of Cape Coast and Anamabu, bought an impounded Dutch ship, *Zorgue,* meaning "care", which the British renamed *Zong*. The outfitting and financial outlay for the *Zong* were part and parcel of a system that brought such economic growth and prosperity to Liverpool that by 1780, it was estimated that as many as eighty-five slavers left Liverpool for the west coast of Africa.

There were already 244 enslaved Africans on board the *Zorgue*, and they became part of the transaction. More Africans were bought in Adja, Agga, Anomabu, the Cape Coast, and the surrounding hinterland of West Africa's Gold Coast (part of modern-day Côte D'Ivoire and Ghana) and placed on board, during the five months before the ship sailed; and under the captaincy of the inexperienced Luke Collingwood, previously the surgeon on the *William*, and a hastily assembled crew, the ship left for Jamaica on 18 August 1781, some 4,000 miles away. Before the Atlantic crossing, it made a stop in São Tomé, leaving there on 6 September 1781 with 442 enslaved people, nineteen crew members (including the first mate, James Kelsall, and second mate, Joseph Wood) and a passenger, Robert Stubbs, a former slaver captain, who would later have to captain the ship temporarily when Collingwood fell ill.

Like most slavers, the *Zong* was overcrowded for its size. At 110 tons, its capacity was 193 people. Its journey was slow, having sailed from further south than most slavers in the eighteenth century. About ten weeks after leaving São Tomé, it arrived in Tobago, after which it continued on its journey to Black River — a total journey of one hundred weeks, according to James Walvin. But not before it veered off-course

*Text box continues*

near Haiti, losing time, before it got back on course for Jamaica. By then, complaints of water shortage, illness and death among the crew and poor navigational and leadership decisions all created a level of confusion aboard. Added to this, towards the end of November, many of the Africans – around 62 – had started to die from disease and malnutrition. Recall that the 244 already on board when the ship was resold had endured an inordinately long period in the hold; and no one knows how long before that they had been on board.

With the captain and crew arguing that water and rations would not last for everyone on board before arrival in Jamaica, the decision was taken to jettison some Africans in order to avoid more deaths, which would threaten the profitability of the journey and would allow the possibility of claiming insurance for "lost cargo". The deposition by chief mate Colonel James Kelsall detailed how Collingwood met with his crew to outline his murderous plans. At 8:00 p.m. on 29 November 1781, 54 enslaved Africans, mainly women and children, were dragged from below deck, unshackled and heaved from the ship through the cabin window, singly, into the ocean. Two days later, on 1 December, 42 men were thrown overboard, handcuffed and in irons, from the quarterdeck. A third batch of 36 (some sources say 38) were murdered later. Many struggled and the crew had to tie iron balls to their ankles to drown them. Another 10 Africans threw themselves overboard in what has been described as an "act of defiance". One man was said to have scrambled back on board to plead with the crew to stop the killings but his pleas obviously fell on deaf ears. More Africans (around 36) were to die before the ship reached Jamaica. Tragically, when the *Zong* arrived in Black River on 22 December 1781, with the bodies of some of the dead Africans still on board, only 208 out of the 442 had survived the voyage. A newspaper reported on 9 January 1782 that 200 of the survivors were soon advertised for sale. I wonder what happened to those dead bodies?

That was not the end of the case of the *Zong*. James Gregson filed an insurance claim on behalf of the owners for the dead enslaved Africans. The insurance initially taken out on the ship included £8,000 for the captives alone, at around £30 sterling per enslaved African. The initial case was heard in March 1782, when Gregson argued that the *Zong* had not had enough water to sustain both crew and the enslaved. That and the fear of insurrection influenced the decision to jettison some of the "cargo" using the maritime law of general average. The insurance underwriter, Thomas Gilbert, in disputing the claim, argued that the *Zong* had 420 gallons of water aboard when she was inventoried in Jamaica. Despite this, the jury in 1782 (under the direction of William Murray, the Earl of Mansfield and the lord chief justice of the King's Bench) found in favour of the owners, and instructed the insurers to pay compensation to the Gregson syndicate.

*Text box continues*

The insurers appealed the case in 1783, with Lord Mansfield himself presiding in the highest court in Britain on 21–22 May of that year, flanked by Mr Justice Buller and Mr Justice Willes. Among those who testified was Great Britain's solicitor general, Justice John Lee, who claimed that property, not people, had been thrown overboard the *Zong*. He is reported to have said: "What is this claim that human people have been thrown overboard? This is a case of chattels or goods. Blacks are goods and property; it is madness to accuse these well-serving honourable men of murder. . . . The case is the same as if wood had been thrown overboard."

These sentiments incensed many people, provoked a great deal of public interest and intensified the campaign for abolition by Equiano, Granville Sharpe and others. Nevertheless, at the end of the review of the evidence and the legal documents, and especially because at this trial it was revealed for the first time that the Africans were thrown overboard a day after a shower of rain relieved the water shortage, no compensation was given to the owners. A retrial was ordered by Mansfield and his colleagues; but according to James Walvin, there is no evidence that it took place, though the legal wranglings, like the transatlantic trafficking in enslaved Africans by many, including the Gregson syndicate, went on. But so did the fight for abolition, emancipation and memorialization.

The essence of the legal proceedings was not criminal liability for the deaths of 132 Africans; rather, it was the liability of the insurers that was in question. This was the most appalling and sordid part of the entire proceedings. Even more gut-wrenching was the pronouncement by Chief Justice Mansfield, who is widely acclaimed as bringing justice to freed blacks in England (in the 1772 Somerset case), that the case before the jury was whether it was necessary that the Africans were thrown into the sea, for he had no doubt that *"the case of slaves was the same as if horses had been thrown overboard"*.

Unfortunately, the murder of Africans on slavers to the Americas was not confined to the *Zong*. There were cases before and after the *Zong*. Before the *Zong* there was the Dutch ship *Leusden*, which on its final voyage ended in the single largest human tragedy in Dutch maritime history. The ship departed from Elmina in modern-day Ghana on 19 November 1737. On board were seven hundred African captives, destined to be sold into enslavement in Surinam. On 1 January 1738, the *Leusden* got into difficulties at the mouth of the Maroni River in Surinam. The crew and sixteen Africans on deck escaped alive; but before departing, the crew deliberately nailed shut the hatches on to the deck so that the other imprisoned captives below could not escape. Over six hundred Africans were left to die below deck, either from drowning or suffocation.

---

Summarized from James Walvin, *The* Zong: *A Massacre, the Law and the End of Slavery* (New Haven: Yale University Press, 2011).

The legitimization of the enslaved as chattel or property was used to justify two of the most cynical aspects of the Emancipation Act, passed in 1833 to come into effect in 1834. First was the apprenticeship system that was meant to last for six years, from 1834 to 1840 (but cut short in 1838), during which the formerly enslaved, it was argued, would learn to operate as free agents and as preparation for full freedom. In reality, apprenticeship was a form of compensation for enslavers: it provided them with access to the free labour of their "property" in the formerly enslaved, in lieu of monetary compensation amounting to £27 million, to which they argued they were entitled. This £27 million in the form of the apprenticeship system was in addition to the £20 million paid out to enslavers by the British government as compensation for the loss of their "property". The enslaved were never compensated; neither were their descendants, who for several generations have continued to suffer from the legacies of the worst crime in human history.

Kris Manjapra of Tufts University, in the United States, tells us that of the £20 million, £15 million was acquired through a loan from the Rothschild syndicate in 1835, with the government supplying £5 million thereafter. This total was gradually repaid to these lenders over the next 180 years, with interest, by taxes collected from the British public, including people from the Caribbean, who as descendants of the formerly enslaved were in fact being asked to pay twice. Incredibly, this bond was not finally paid off until 2015. Twenty million pounds might not seem like a lot of money today, but in 1835 it represented 40 per cent of the government's expenditure. According to Manjapra, the amount is equivalent to over £200 billion today; other people say this equivalent is just over £17 billion.

The extent of the greed and moral degradation of the Caribbean enslavers and their allies in the British government is the revelation that they received compensation not just for enslaved Africans present on plantations and other properties at the time of Emancipation but for those who had run away, long absent from the fields, those who had bought their freedom, and even for some who were long dead. As Manjapra expresses it:

It is a gruesome experience to sit in the archives of the United Kingdom and to turn the pages of dusty archival documents reeking in mildew, negligence and racial terrorization as 800,000 black people were transformed into twenty million pounds of financial value and distributed to more than 44,441 slave owning claimants. And the ready cash to carry out this necromantic transubstantiation of slaves – living, absent and dead – into money acquired through the raising of a massive loan by the British government in 1835 that the British state continued to pay for almost two centuries, ending only in 2015.[18]

## Deceptive Indentureship

The CRC has included the case of post-slavery indentured Asian Indians in the Caribbean to the list of people for whom reparation from Europeans is due. After 1838, planters in the Caribbean lobbied for immigrant labourers from Asia to supplement the labour force. There continues to be controversy, however, over whether or not the Caribbean had really needed additional labourers after Emancipation or the planters simply had to pay higher wages to attract freed Africans as well as offering them better working conditions and improved labour relations. The only countries in the Caribbean that conceivably needed additional labourers, if they were to continue the sugar industry, were Trinidad (now Trinidad and Tobago), British Guiana and Surinam. Trinidad and British Guiana were developed late as sugar economies and just as they were expanding the industry, the 1807 act to stop trading in Africans was passed. Of course, they could have made the choice to use the labour available to engage in other economic activities. As this was not the choice they made, they lobbied for additional labourers from India and China. Jamaica, Barbados and other parts of the Caribbean could have managed without imported labourers, but immigration was not only about the need for labourers, it was also about economic control. Planters were, therefore, able to convince Britain and other

---

18. Kris Manjapra, "Necrospeculation: Postemancipation Finance and Black Redress", *Social Text* 37, no. 2 (2019): 44.

European powers, like the French and the Dutch, to facilitate Asian indentured migration to the region.

There are those who view the system of Asian indentured migration as purely voluntary. This is not true. There were many aspects of the process that were deceptive, especially when it concerned the recruitment of Indian women. The system was marked by kidnapping, unclear contractual arrangements, breaches of contracts and failure to fulfil the contractual obligations for repatriation, the cost of which increasingly fell on the Indians themselves. The crew did not always abide by the regulations onboard the ships that transported Asians to the Caribbean and there are documented cases, for example in Shepherd's *Maharani's Misery*, of the rape and death of Indian women on their passage to the Caribbean. There were oppressive aspects of indentureship on Caribbean plantations and even though land was promised, in lieu of repatriation, many Indians complained about the nonarable nature of such lands. While Chinese indentureship lasted a very short time, except for the case of Cuba, and the numbers were small, with many buying themselves out of indentureship, the immigration of Indians to the Caribbean lasted from 1838 to 1917. The deceptive aspects of the entire system, along with the oppressive nature of plantation agriculture and living conditions, provide a basis for Asians in the Caribbean to be included in the reparatory justice movement.

## The Perpetrators

The main focus of the reparation movement is on the following countries which were involved in the illegal trafficking of enslaved Africans: Britain, Denmark, France, Portugal, Spain and the Netherlands, with Britain and Portugal accounting for the majority of those trafficked. However, our knowledge of the extent and varied nature of European participation, as well as the statistics on the number of Africans trafficked, has been considerably enhanced by an important resource in the Slave Voyages Database.[19] The

---

19. Slave Voyages Database, https://www.slavevoyages.org/.

database brings together the work of scholars all over the world, led by David Eltis and a team originally based at Emory University in the United States. In its latest version, the Slave Voyages Database 2.0 of 2018 tracks the movements of ships, the countries to which they belonged, the number of people who were forcibly taken from Africa to the Americas, and the ports at which they disembarked. This resource has allowed us to expand the list of perpetrators to include the United States, Sweden, Switzerland, Norway, Germany and Belgium. Others will be added as the research progresses. We now know that the total number of voyages stands at 36,000, but it is equally significant to have evidence that other European countries not previously identified were participants, whether by transporting Africans themselves, investing in companies that transported Africans, establishing plantations, or manufacturing goods that serviced trafficking. Based on the work of Hans Fässler[20] of Switzerland and Jan Lönn of Sweden, two examples are Switzerland, which provided financing and actually manufactured the precision instruments that guided slavers, and Sweden, which supplied the iron that was manufactured into the instruments of torture in factories, such as those in Birmingham.

## The Beneficiaries

From a British-colonized Caribbean perspective, the United Kingdom and its institutions were the greatest beneficiaries of the illegal trade in Africans and slavery. The Industrial Revolution would have been impossible without the wealth generated by enslaved labour. Britain's major ports, cities and canals were built on invested money generated by the labour of enslaved people. Several banks can trace their origins to the financing of the TTA: Barclays (then known as the Colonial Bank), Barings and HSBC, which can be traced back to Thomas Leyland's banking house. The Bank of England and the Bank of Scotland both had close connections to the trade, and the

---

20. Hans Fässler, "Venus without Nose: Switzerland as a Colonial Player in the Caribbean" (presentation at the symposium "Western Banking, Colonialism and Reparations", Jolly Beach Hotel, Antigua and Barbuda, 10 October 2019).

House of Rothschild, in cooperation with the British Treasury, was the principal actor in the floating of the £20 million bond that was raised to compensate enslavers for the loss of their "property" at Emancipation.[21] Hundreds of Britain's imposing houses were built with the wealth of slavery and the Church of England has also acknowledged its pecuniary gains from slavery. Universities such as Bristol, Cambridge, Edinburgh, Glasgow and Oxford all benefited from slavery profits. Several of these British universities have established committees or working groups to research their connection to slavery and consider reparatory justice actions. The most advanced is the University of Glasgow, which initiated a project to research its past connection with Caribbean slavery and published its findings.[22]

There is no denying the fact that royal families throughout Europe developed financial interests in the TTA, and monarchs – among them King Louis XVI of France, King George I of England, King Christian IV of Denmark and King Gustav of Sweden – had a mutual interest in the trade's prosperity. King Christian IV, in fact, invested 16,000 rixdaler in the East India Company and became a major shareholder in the business of African enslavement. With royal patronage and the need to ensure a return on investment, the level of organization that went into the capture and subsequent enslavement of Africans was unmatched. State-sponsored companies, such as Denmark-Norway's Royal Chartered Danish West India–Guinea Company, were also granted exclusive licences to operate in the trans-shipment of millions of enslaved Africans.

The British royal family invested heavily in the Royal African Company, and King James II became chairman of the board of directors of what was at that time the largest slave trading company in

---

21. Jasper Jolly, "Barclays, HSBC and Lloyds among UK Banks That Had Links to Slavery", *Guardian*, 18 June 2020, https://www.theguardian.com/business/2020/jun/18/barclays-hsbc-and-lloyds-among-uk-banks-that-had-links-to-slavery; Kris Manjapra, "When Will Britain Face up to Its Crimes against Humanity?", *Guardian*, 29 March 2018, https://www.theguardian.com/news/2018/mar/29/slavery-abolition-compensation-when-will-britain-face-up-to-its-crimes-against-humanity.

22. "Reparation for Slavery at Last", *Jamaica Global*, 31 July 2019, https://www.jamaicaglobalonline.com/reparation-for-slavery-at-last/.

the world. The wealth generated was passed down from generation through generation to the current royal family of Queen Elizabeth II, queen of Jamaica and a number of other CARICOM countries that remain in the Commonwealth. The beneficiaries also included parliamentarians. It is estimated that in 1776, forty members of the British Parliament were making their money from investments in the Caribbean and, in total, over a hundred members of Parliament in the British House of Commons had a direct link to slavery and the trade in enslaved Africans.

Like the Slave Voyages Database, the Centre for the Study of Legacies of British Slavery at University College London has created an important database which carries the record of 46,000 Britons who received compensation.[23] Between 10 and 15 per cent of the nineteenth-century elite had connections with slave ownership. Many notable people in contemporary British society, including former prime minister David Cameron, have been identified as descendants of people who benefited from slavery.[24] The value of the database, in the words of its former director Nicholas Draper, is that it brings to light previously unknown or unacknowledged connections between the owners of enslaved people and firms, families and institutions that have contributed to the formation of modern Britain. An updated version of the database also tracks the ownership histories of estates in the Caribbean at the time of Emancipation, compiled from the records of the compensation paid to enslavers, making it possible to identify all enslavers in the British-colonized Caribbean at the time slavery ended.

---

23. Legacies of British Slave-Ownership, Centre for the Study of the Legacies of British Slavery, University College London, https://www.ucl.ac.uk/lbs.

24. Sam Jones, "Follow the Money: Investigators Trace Forgotten Story of Britain's Slave Trade", *Guardian*, 27 August 2013, https://www.theguardian.com/world/2013/aug/27/britain-slave-trade.

The rest of this chapter elaborates on the specific reasons that several European countries are being singled out for reparatory justice. We begin with Spain, the United Kingdom, Portugal, France, and the Netherlands, then we focus on Denmark, Sweden, Norway, Germany and Switzerland.

## Spain's Reparation Debt to the Caribbean

Spain, the first European country to colonize the Caribbean, played an indisputable role in the decimation of the Indigenous Peoples who were the owners of the lands of the Caribbean and Latin America. Spain sold Africans into slavery. Spain maintained a brutal system of enslavement in places like Cuba, Puerto Rico, the Dominican Republic and Jamaica. Spain systematically extracted wealth from the region to develop its own society and unwillingly abolished slavery. Spain compensated some planters who claimed state settlement for the loss of the African labour force at Emancipation but made no provisions to assist the freed people to manage their lives. Spain devastated the physical environment, for example through plantation construction, making the region today more susceptible to the impact of climate change. The legacies of Spain's past actions still linger in the Caribbean among the descendants of Indigenous Peoples and enslaved Africans.

## The United Kingdom's Reparation Debt to the Caribbean

The United Kingdom unquestionably played a significant role in the death and destruction of Indigenous Peoples and societies in the Caribbean. This is especially evident in the Eastern Caribbean territories of Dominica, Grenada, St Vincent and the Grenadines, and St Lucia. These deaths were not only a result of diseases brought to the islands by outsiders, including the British, but also a result of a systematic and intentional war for their lands, which lasted over a hundred years.

Britain then continued the harm through its active, instrumental and demonstrable participation in the enslavement of approximately

3.2 million Africans (about 26 per cent of that figure traded to the Americas), many of whom were kidnapped and forcibly relocated to CARICOM member states by royal decree. This practice continued for nearly three hundred years and fuelled the economy of the United Kingdom. In fact, UK member of Parliament Diane Abbott reminded her parliamentary colleagues in 2007 that fifteen lord mayors, twenty-five sheriffs and thirty-eight aldermen were shareholders in the Royal African Company.[25] During these centuries, the labour of Africans, combined with the resources of the region, was harnessed for Britain's development, leaving Africa and the Caribbean severely underdeveloped. When sustained opposition by the enslaved and abolitionist campaigns in Europe finally brought down the system of slavery, planters were compensated by the British government while the freed people were left with nothing but freedom and no plan for their reparation and repatriation.

The harm to the region's people was further compounded by the practice of moving migrant labourers, the majority from southeast Asia, under indentureship to supplement the post-slavery labour force on plantations and other enterprises owned and managed by British planters on the false pretence of decent contracts and conditions of work. Indeed, the view that Asian migration in particular was completely voluntary is a myth (as noted in chapter 2), with evidence existing that many, especially women, were tricked into leaving their homelands, some never to return.

## Portugal's Reparation Debt to the Caribbean

Portugal's involvement had broad impact on the Americas and the Atlantic World. Portugal played a significant role in the decimation of some of the Indigenous Peoples of the Americas (for example, in Brazil) and the creation of the Atlantic economy, which evolved to include the TTA.

Indeed, Portugal is estimated to have accounted for almost 50

---

25. Statement delivered by Diane Abbott in the House of Commons, Hansard, Debates, 20 March 2007, https://publications.parliament.uk/pa/cm200607/cmhansrd/cm070320/debtext/70320-0007.htm.

per cent of the Africans trafficked across the Atlantic.[26] The Portuguese trade was not confined to the places it colonized directly; it extended outside its large former colony of Brazil to CARICOM member states, including Suriname, Jamaica, Barbados and Guyana.

## France's Reparation Debt to the Caribbean

France, like other European states, such as England, Spain and Portugal, played an instrumental role in the genocide of Indigenous Peoples in the Caribbean and the enslavement of Africans. This is evident in the treatment of the Kalinagos and the establishment of plantation societies in their various territories, such as Haiti, Guadeloupe and Martinique. France bears responsibility for the genocide of the Kalinagos, the trade in enslaved Africans, and the establishment of a system of oppression for those Africans, known as the *Code Noir*.

In an attempt to acquire the territories in the Eastern Caribbean, the indigenous Kalinagos were dehumanized. An aggressive war was waged against the Kalinagos, in which France attempted to enslave, drive out or exterminate them. The French saw this as necessary to their economic success, which was bound to the capture and enslavement of Indigenous Peoples to provide labour and land. By 1635, France was constantly battling the Kalinagos for control of places such as Guadeloupe. Consequently, between 1492 and 1700, the Kalinago population in the eastern Caribbean fell by 90 per cent. This eventually led to France's genocide of the Indigenous Peoples in that area.

France then focused on the construction of plantation societies. In the early eighteenth century, French traders trafficked approximately 7,500 enslaved Africans per year. After 1737, this increased to approximately 20,000 per year. France is estimated to have trafficked between 1.1 and 1.3 million enslaved Africans in total.[27]

---

26. See Slave Voyages Database, https://www.slavevoyages.org/assessment/estimates.
27. Ibid.

Throughout France's engagement in the trade in enslaved Africans, the former French colony of Haiti/Ayiti (St Domingue) accounted for more than three-quarters of French expeditions to French colonies in the Caribbean and for at least 80 per cent of enslaved Africans sold by the French. By 1715, Haiti had overtaken Martinique as France's prime market for enslaved Africans. In 1790, at the peak of the French trade, French ships landed at least 40,000 Africans in Haiti.

Finally, as early as 1685, the conditions under which the enslaved Africans were subjugated was codified by the creation of the *Code Noir*. This document outlined the treatment of enslaved Africans by the French. In particular, it articulated that they were void of human rights and were to be considered chattel and property. It permitted capital punishment and death penalties for resistance against freed persons, the branding of enslaved Africans, and the inheritance of servitude. As a result, it created an institution where Africans were considered "other". The establishment of plantation economies, the destruction of indigenous communities and the systematic oppression of Africans trafficked to CARICOM member states has left France with a significant debt to the people of the Caribbean.

## The Special Case of Haiti

While the case of Haiti is examined extensively in chapter 3, the specific debt France has to Haiti bears mentioning here as well. In the aftermath of its revolutionary war which resulted in emancipation and independence, the new Haitian nation tried to reconstruct a society and economy. However, France and its allies tried everything in their power to recapture Haiti. In the most blatant example of the impoverishment of a nation, under the 1825 agreement, France forced Haiti to pay 150 million francs, which was then reduced to 90 million francs (about US$21 billion in 2004, according to former Haitian president Jean-Bertrand Aristide) in exchange for France's recognizing it as a sovereign nation. This resulted in the end of the twenty-one years of isolation Haiti faced for having what colonialists regarded as "the audacity" to take its freedom and give freedom to Africans who had been enslaved there. This, however, came at a price as Haiti, after struggling to finally pay off the debt in 1947, has found it difficult to thrive economically and achieve development.[28]

## The Netherlands' Reparation Debt to the Caribbean

The Kingdom of the Netherlands was involved in slavery and the TTA for more than two hundred years. It was responsible for more than five hundred voyages that forced more than 550,000 African men, women and children across the Atlantic. Close to 80,000 died during these voyages.[29] Wealth, income and profits flowed from these activities to hundreds and thousands of Dutch people. An estimate of today's value of the colonial goods imported into the Netherlands and produced by the forced labour of Africans puts the figure at €127 billion. When slavery was legally abolished in the Netherlands in 1863, over 45,000 enslaved Africans in the Dutch-colonized Caribbean became legally free, but, like those in the British-colonized Caribbean, they were required to work without wages for a further period (ten years in the case of the Dutch Caribbean) while the enslavers received close to 12 million guilders in compensation. The total compensation package to enslavers was therefore a combination of financial reward and apprenticeship. The brutality of the Dutch slavery regime (for example, in what is now Guyana and Suriname) is legendary. Dutch sources indicate that the horrifying treatment of the enslaved people was a reason for their resistance. The most significant show of resistance in the eighteenth century was the 1763 Berbice War, at the end of which 124 enslaved people were executed after sentencing by the special court set up to try them by Governor Van Hoogenheim. The reason other enslaved people were returned to their enslavers, from whom they experienced brutal treatment just short of death, was because their labour was deemed important to the economic rehabilitation of the colony.

---

28. Beckles, "Hate and the Quake".
29. See Slave Voyages Database, https://www.slavevoyages.org/.

A century later, the Council for the City of Amsterdam in the Netherlands accepted responsibility for slavery in the Dutch Caribbean by issuing an apology on 24 June 2019. Here is an extract from the *Irish Times* relating to that apology:

> In what's being hailed as a "historic" decision, Amsterdam is to apologise for its role in the slave trade which made it the richest city in the western world for more than 100 years from the mid-17th to mid-18th centuries – creating wealth that remains visible today. . . . Records from the 17th century show that 30 of the city's most prominent merchants were the main drivers behind Dutch slavery, which they developed to a new mass scale. These were men often associated with the magnificent canal houses of the inner city, built to display their wealth. . . . It was during this "golden age" that the Amsterdam stock exchange was established to provide those merchants with a safe and regulated place where they could buy and sell shares in these early globalised enterprises. It is still the oldest functioning stock exchange in the world.[30]

## Denmark's Reparation Debt to the Caribbean

The Kingdom of Denmark is often excluded from the modern discourse on the TTA. Denmark, however, had a role both in the trade of Africans and in the establishment of plantation societies grounded in "slave codes" made to dehumanize and oppress Africans. Denmark, like many European countries at the time, bought and sold enslaved Africans. Denmark's involvement in the then Gold Coast began on 20 April 1663, when it seized the Christiansborg Fort (Osu Castle) and Carlsborg Fort (Cape Castle) as it completed the annexation of Swedish Gold Coast settlements. A number of trading stations and forts were built by the Danes during their time in what is now Ghana, several of which are in ruins today. Osu Castle

---

30. Peter Cluskey, "Amsterdam to Apologise for Role in Slave Trade", *Irish Times*, 25 June 2019, https://www.irishtimes.com/news/world/europe/amsterdam-to-apologise-for-role-in-slave-trade-1.3937384. This apology was officially made on 1 July 2021 by the mayor of Amsterdam (see https://www.bbc.com/news/world-europe-57680209).

was the base for Danish power in West Africa and the centre for the TTA to the Danish Caribbean. Despite the shorter period of active transatlantic trade in enslaved Africans by Denmark, it is estimated that 85,000 enslaved Africans were transported to the Danish Caribbean.[31]

The Danish West India Company, established in 1671, was based on the rationale that colonization yielded economic benefits. Hence, it established a colonial plantation society.[32] By 1700, there were 122 plantations; by 1715, there were 160, with thirty-two operational sugar mills and more than 3,000 enslaved Africans. The Danish private trading companies used the Caribbean islands to accrue and generate profits in a trade of enslaved Africans from the Gold Coast. To maintain the system of chattel slavery on which Danish Caribbean plantation economy depended, the minority European community created a mechanism of superior force. The ultimate manifestations of that force lay with the military and the power of the state to inflict pain on the bodies of the enslaved as well as the laws which accompanied this force.

### Sweden's Reparation Debt to the Caribbean

Sweden's participation began on 12 May 1646, when a Swedish expedition sailed to Africa on the initiative of businessman Louis de Geer. State-sponsored companies like his were granted licences to operate in the TTA. From what is today Nigeria, the expedition sailed from Africa with 260 Africans, all of whom were sent to Barbados. Only 150 of them were alive when the ship arrived.

In 1650, Sweden established trading stations along the West African coast. One example was Fort Carlsborg, with bases in an area called the Swedish Gold Coast, later the West African Gold Coast, which is today part of modern Ghana. It was only in 1663

---

31. See Slave Voyages Database, https://www.slavevoyages.org/assessment/estimates.

32. Scott Stawski, "Denmark's veiled role in Slavery in the Americas: The Impact of the Danish West Indies on the Transatlantic Slave Trade" (master's thesis, Harvard Extension School, 2018), 34–35.

that Denmark took over the Swedish Gold Coast, which was then renamed the Danish Gold Coast. But while it lasted, the Swedish Gold Coast was a profitable colony. Swedes were also responsible for the construction of Cape Coast Castle in Ghana, one of the barracoons where captured Africans were held before shipment. Sources on Sweden's participation in the TTA and African enslavement tell a tale of cruelty and racism that any modern nation should admit outright and condemn as a reprehensible part of its history.

Rulers and others in Sweden were enriched by their participation in the trafficking in enslaved Africans and African enslavement – even national heroes such as Gustav III, Queen Kristina, Axel Oxenstierna and Louis de Geer. This means that, contrary to Sweden's public pronouncements and positions today, it is built partly on the backs of enslaved Africans and their descendants still suffer as a result.

Sweden was not a major colonizer in the same way as Britain, France, Spain, Portugal, Denmark and the Netherlands in terms of territories invaded, settled and exploited. Sweden, however, colonized St Barthelemy in the Caribbean between 1784 and 1878 and used it as a free port and a major centre for the TTA, because plantation agriculture would not have made the island economically profitable. In 1786, Sweden went further and established the Swedish West India Company, which was granted the right to trade in enslaved Africans between Africa and the Caribbean. Shares were sold in this company, with King Gustav reserving 10 per cent of the shares for himself.

Africans were kidnapped and forcibly relocated to the Caribbean by royal decree. They were trafficked tax-free by foreign vessels, after which the Swedish king made a profit by collecting an export tax when the enslaved peoples who were bought were shipped out.

Sweden was also a major supplier of iron used in the TTA.[33] Scholars indicate that during the sixteenth century, Sweden exported

---

33. Catherine Edwards, "The Little-Known Role Sweden Played in the Colonial Slave Trade", *Local*, 15 June 2020, https://www.thelocal.se/20200615/how-can-sweden-better-face-up-to-its-colonial-past/.

more iron than any other country and the British, in particular, were dependent on Swedish iron in order to make instruments of torture, such as shackles. The country also signed treaties with Britain and France and itself had slavers involved in the TTA. This implicates Sweden and affected not only St Barthelemy, while under the country's jurisdiction, but also other CARICOM member states.

### Norway's Reparation Debt to the Caribbean

It is not well known that Norway played an active role in the TTA. Although Norway was under Danish and Swedish rule during the sixteenth to nineteenth centuries, and the sovereignty of Norway was under the Danish crown, the Norwegian people still demonstrated varying degrees of participation. Indeed, at the time of the system of African enslavement, Norwegians as a distinct group were participants in the TTA.

Norway provided ports, such as Narestø near the east side of Tranøy, and Norwegians contributed to staffing ports and vessels, all of which were essential for the TTA. There were approximately three thousand voyages made between the Kingdom of Denmark-Norway and the Caribbean, resulting in the trafficking of around 85,000 enslaved Africans to CARICOM member states.

The Norwegian ship the *Fredensborg* is just one example of this explicit participation. Not only was the *Fredensborg* used to trade enslaved Africans, but the outports of Norway were also extremely important in the trafficking of the enslaved. During the first five voyages of the *Fredensborg*, three of the winters were spent in Norway. The ship was built in Copenhagen, Denmark; its first voyage in 1756 arrived in the Danish Caribbean with 200 Africans, only one third of the original 600 captured.

Norwegians made up around 10 per cent of the total crew serving on slavers at any one time and the TTA was considered a large economic activity. They staffed forts on the African coast, sailed on the ships and carried goods produced by the enslaved back to Norway and the rest of Europe. Those Norwegians who served at the posts on the Gold Coast came from various backgrounds and were soldiers, gunsmiths, artisans and even clergymen.

There were even Norwegians in high-ranking positions in Africa during the time of the enslavement of Africans. Andreas Wellemsen was governor at Christiansborg (the capital of the Danish Gold Coast) during the Akwamu war (1727–1730), one of the bloodiest conflicts in the Gold Coast's history. Using his position, Wellemsen managed to secure Danish-Norwegian trade interests by both avoiding war and securing a high number of African prisoners of war. Another Norwegian, Søren Schielderup, also served as governor at the fort at Christiansborg (1735–1736).[34] Hence, Norway's imprint is evident at all levels of the TTA. The overall societal participation of Norwegian citizens within the TTA warrants responsibility and reparatory justice.

## The Federal Republic of Germany's Reparation Debt to the Caribbean

Germany played an active role in the TTA. Although there was no German state until 1871, citizens of what is now Germany helped to finance the trade and bought and sold Africans to the British and the French. When "Germany" is used, it should be with that awareness in mind. Brandenburg-Prussia (now part of Germany) also participated in the TTA in the seventeenth century. Affluent merchant families, such as the Welsers and Fuggers from Augsburg, also received important trading privileges. They were bankers to the Spanish crown who were significant participants in the TTA. The Welsers brought some 4,000 enslaved Africans from Cape Verde and São Tomé via Seville or took them directly to the Americas. They also owned sugar plantations in Hispaniola (the Dominican Republic and Haiti) that used significant numbers of enslaved African labourers. Additionally, there were also failed attempts to establish a plantation economy in Germany's Caribbean colonies in the Virgin Islands.

In an attempt to emulate the Dutch West India Company, Elector Friedrich Wilhelm of Brandenburg in the early 1680s also began to

---

34. Audrey Andersen, "Slave Trading Past Still Haunts Norway", *Newsinenglish.no*, 28 September 2014, https://www.newsinenglish.no/2014/09/28/slave-trading-past-still-haunts-norway/.

engage in this trade. He constructed harbours for oceangoing vessels and built and purchased ships, many of which sailed for the Gulf of Guinea. Agents of the Brandenburg state sold some 10,000 to 30,000 enslaved Africans to America. German states, such as Hamburg, also outfitted ships and sent them to Africa.

In addition to Groß-Friedrichsburg on the Gold Coast, Brandenburg and Prussia acquired two more overseas bases to facilitate the trade. The Caribbean island of St Thomas was also used as a "reloading point" for the resale of enslaved Africans to the British and the French. All this contributed to the success of Germany's Brandenburgisch-Afrikanische Compagnie.

Eventually, the business of trading Africans expanded to the wider population of Brandenburg-Prussia. In the seventeenth, eighteenth and nineteenth centuries, German ships, sailors and captains from Friesland, Hamburg, Bremen and Schleswig took part in the TTA. In 1682 and 1683, Otto Friedrich von der Groeben was able to establish two trading posts in West Africa, Fort Groß-Friedrichsburg and Fort Dorothea, further illustrating German involvement in the TTA.

With royal patronage and the need to ensure a return on investment, the level of organization that went into the capture and subsequent enslavement of Africans was unmatched. State-sponsored companies, such as Germany's Brandenburgisch-Afrikanische Compagnie, were also granted exclusive licences to operate in the trans-shipment of millions of enslaved Africans.[35]

## Switzerland's Reparation Debt to the Caribbean

Admittedly, Switzerland did not exist as a discrete nation state at the time of the trafficking in enslaved Africans; neither was it considered a European imperial power. It did not have colonies in the Americas nor did it have a plantation economy. There were no bustling port cities, because of its geographic location as a landlocked state.

---

35. Heike Raphael-Hernandez and Pia Wiegmink, "German Entanglements in Transatlantic Slavery: An Introduction", *Atlantic Studies* 14, no. 4 (2017): 419–35.

Usually, this narrative provides an escape from the assumption of a nation having participated in the Atlantic economy built on the TTA. However, Switzerland's geographical location, along with its intertwined history with Germany and France, has left it with an irrefutable role in the TTA, mainly in the areas of supplying precision navigational instruments to slavers as well as through banking and finance and the establishment of companies to trade Africans. Swiss banks played an instrumental role in financing many voyages throughout the Atlantic. Switzerland owned as much as one third of the Compagnie des Indes, a French company that held a monopoly over the West African trade. Further, between 1719 and 1734, the city of Bern owned shares in the British South Sea Company, which sold enslaved Africans in the Americas. Bern was by far the largest shareholder, exceeding the Bank of England and King George I.[36] Other involvement is clear: from 1783 to 1818, Swiss companies Christoph Burckhardt & Sohn, Christoph Burckhardt & Cie, and Bourcard Fils & Cie took part in twenty-one expeditions for enslaved Africans. Some of its citizens were among the crew on slavers and others fought to suppress resistance movements of enslaved Africans, in particular the Haitian Revolution.

---

36. Fässler, "Venus without Nose".

Table 2.1. Summary of voyages under the flags of European colonial powers that travelled to the Caribbean

| Country/Flag | Number of Voyages | Year Range | Place of Embarkation | Place of Disembarkation | Total Embarked | Total Disembarked | Mortality Rate |
| --- | --- | --- | --- | --- | --- | --- | --- |
| Denmark | 194 | 1646–1823 | Africa | Caribbean | 48,954 | 41,238 | 15.76% |
| France | 3,234 | 1575–1864 | Africa | Caribbean | 1,055,368 | 913,728 | 13.42% |
| Great Britain | 8,837 | 1563–1808 | Africa | Caribbean | 2,454,939 | 2,106,655 | 14.19% |
| Portugal | 314 | 1532–1859 | Africa | Caribbean | 114,060 | 100,398 | 11.98% |
| Spain | 1,125 | 1526–1863 | Africa | Caribbean | 349,976 | 308,753 | 11.78% |
| Sweden | 12 | 1646–1820 | Africa | Caribbean | 1,802 | 1,562 | 13.32% |
| The Netherlands | 1,003 | 1606–1829 | Africa | Caribbean | 371,634 | 324,001 | 12.82% |

*Source:* Slave Voyages Database 2.0, https://slavevoyages.org/.

Table 2.2. Extract of slavers that trafficked enslaved Africans to the Caribbean

| Country/Flag | Vessel Name | Principal Place of Purchase | Place of Disembarkation | Total Embarked | Total Disembarked | Year of Arrival |
|---|---|---|---|---|---|---|
| Denmark | Christianus Quintus (a) Christian V | Christiansborg | St Thomas | 447 | 393 | 1707 |
| Denmark | Mercurius | Bight of Benin, port unspecified | St Croix | 73 | 62 | 1756 |
| Great Britain | Isabel | Calabar | Barbados, port unspecified | 251 | 174 | 1646 |
| Great Britain | Desire | Calabar | St John (Antigua) | 199 | 138 | 1678 |
| Portugal | Cleópatra | Saint-Louis | Jamaica, port unspecified | 135 | 120 | 1805 |
| Portugal | S Salvador | Luanda | Hispaniola, unspecified | 359 | 287 | 1604 |
| Spain | Pez Volador | Africa, port unspecified | Santiago de Cuba | 83 | 73 | 1809 |
| Spain | Concepción | Cape Verde Islands | Puerto Rico, port unspecified | 325 | 260 | 1527 |
| Sweden | Neptuno | Africa, port unspecified | Havana | 123 | 98 | 1797 |
| Sweden | Onlyfer | Africa, port unspecified | St Barthelemy, port unspecified | 124 | 101 | 1805 |
| The Netherlands | Gideon | Portudal | Curaçao | 385 | 331 | 1659 |
| The Netherlands | Goude Poort | Loango | Surinam | 524 | 477 | 1675 |
| United States | America | Africa, port unspecified | Havana | 264 | 226 | 1790 |
| United States | Friend's Adventure | Gambia | Barbados, port unspecified | – | 142 | 1730 |

*Source*: Slave Voyages Database 2.0, https://slavevoyages.org/.

## Conclusion

Based on the evidence presented in this chapter, there is no denying the deep involvement of former colonial powers in indigenous genocide, the TTA and chattel enslavement. The European countries of Spain, the United Kingdom, Portugal, France, the Netherlands, Denmark, Sweden, Norway, Germany, and Switzerland all have a case to answer. The unfinished business is for them to follow apologies and statements of regret by engaging in a reparatory settlement with the Caribbean for the crimes of indigenous genocide, the TTA, chattel enslavement and deceptive Asian indentureship.

# 3

# Setting Out the Caribbean Case for Reparation

The case for reparation rests on sound legal, moral and economic grounds and there is precedent for reparation settlements. This chapter sets out the economic, moral, biblical and legal case for reparation in the Caribbean context.

## The Economic Case

Former prime minister of Trinidad and Tobago Eric Williams has provided the handbook for the economic case for reparation in his seminal work *Capitalism and Slavery*, an examination of how the institution of slavery led to the development of British capitalism. In his work, Williams elucidates the fact that the Caribbean played an integral role in the accumulation of capital that led to the modern-day United Kingdom. He traces the profits generated from the TTA and slavery to the development of financial institutions in the United Kingdom, including Barclays, the Bank of Scotland, Heywood, HSBC and Lloyds, showing that the founders of and stakeholders in these institutions were merchants and investors in the TTA, owners of plantations in the Caribbean, and oftentimes providers of insurance for enslaved people and slavers. It is these profits earned that led to the rise of these modern-day financial institutions.

Yet profits from the TTA and slavery were not limited only to these contemporary banks. In fact, money accumulated from the forced labour of enslaved Africans in the Caribbean can be traced to the enrichment of wealthy families in the United Kingdom, such as the Beckford and Gladstone families. This money can also be traced to the development of cities in the United Kingdom, including Birmingham, Bristol, Edinburgh, Glasgow, Liverpool, London and Manchester. Williams also argues that capitalism quickly replaced the institution of slavery only after profits accumulated from slavery and the TTA were substantial enough to fund the British industrial revolution.

Even before Williams had articulated his economic rationale for reparation, Sir Arthur Lewis, in his book *Labour in the West Indies*, had justified why he believed that Britain had a reparatory justice case to answer: "What claim have West Indians to demand such sacrifices from the British people? Briefly this. It is the British who, by their action in past centuries, are responsible for the presence in these islands of the majority of their inhabitants, whose ancestors as slaves contributed millions to the wealth of Great Britain, a debt which the British have yet to repay."[37]

In negotiating for a "golden handshake", similar to what Britain gave its Asian colonies (the Colombo Plan[38] in 1950), the first negotiators for Caribbean independence from Jamaica and Trinidad and Tobago reinforced the responsibility of Britain to make an economic investment in a region it had underdeveloped. Jamaica asked for £40 million but only got £2 million. Trinidad and Tobago expressed its disappointment at Britain's refusal to vote a respectable sum to enable the twin-island nation to actualize its independence, especially as there was a caveat that even the small sum granted had to be used to buy British goods. Williams was the only postcolonial leader initially to refuse the offer, claiming the quantum insufficient, the

---

37. W. Arthur Lewis, *Labour in the West Indies: The Birth of a Workers' Movement* (1939; repr., London: New Beacon, 1977).
38. "The History of Colombo Plan", https://colombo-plan.org/history/.

attached strings an insult, and the offer itself "invoking the spectre of colonial exploitation and its relationship to the construction of the British economy". In an address to the students at the London School of Economics in 1962, Williams stated, "The West Indies are in the position of an orange. The British have sucked it dry and their sole concern today is that they should not slip and get damaged on the peel.... The offer is quite unacceptable and we would prefer not to have it ... [it] amounted to aid to Britain rather than to Trinidad. ... I do not propose to accept any concept of the Commonwealth which means common wealth for Britain and common poverty for us."[39] Williams eventually accepted this grant, but he became a thorn in Britain's side thereafter.

Lewis and Williams gave a clear depiction of how the forced and unpaid labour of Africans in the Caribbean directly led to the enrichment and development of European nations and of these nations' refusal to provide substantial financial support, even at independence. By doing so, they provided the framework to argue for the need for economic reparation for the descendants of those enslaved Africans in the Caribbean.

## The Moral Case

### The Brutality of Conquest and Colonization

There is no denying the brutality of the European conquest and colonization of the Caribbean and its original inhabitants. Upon their encounter with the Indigenous Peoples of the Caribbean, European colonizers violently ripped away their livelihood and lands. They attempted to enslave the Indigenous Peoples, who were forced to work to enrich European coffers with the proceeds. The colonizers' demand that the Indigenous Peoples cultivate food both for their own communities and for Europeans was a burdensome one that resulted in starvation for the Indigenous Peoples. The colonizers further contributed to the displacement of the Indigenous

---

39. Colin A. Palmer, *Eric Williams and the Making of the Modern Caribbean* (Chapel Hill: University of North Carolina Press, 2006), 149.

Peoples by moving them from one part of the Caribbean to another as labour needs grew in specific places with reduced populations. Those who resisted and refused to work for the Europeans were violently killed. The numbers from historical records paint a chilling picture. As explained in chapter 2, there was a drastic reduction in the preconquest population throughout the region, in particular affecting the Taino and Kalinago/Garifuna populations.[40]

## Treatment under the System of African Enslavement

Once they had almost completely eliminated the Indigenous Peoples of the Caribbean, whose populations only slowly recovered over time, the Europeans turned to chattel enslavement and the TTA to supply the labour force. The brutality inflicted is incomparable. African men, women and children were ripped from their homes and families and forced to undergo a horrendous journey across the Atlantic to a completely foreign world. Africans were introduced to the repugnant evil of chattel slavery, an institution in which Europeans perceived Africans to be property, with no human dignity and rights. This gave way to Africans being bought and sold, branded and bred like animals, mortgaged, invested, rented, replaced when their value depreciated, and brutalized. Chattel slavery was racially defined and attached only to Africans, who were forced to work long hours daily, frequently whipped, and imprisoned or executed for any signs of resistance.

The Europeans brutalized the enslaved Africans, and women bore the brunt of this brutality. Forced to act as the backbone of the labour force in the fields (they were the majority in the field gangs), often separated from their young ones, African women were also subjected to the violent sexual exploitation of European men. They were often sexually abused, as seen, for example, in the writings of Thomas Thistlewood, Robert Wedderburn and others. Wedderburn, the son of an enslaved woman and a white planter, stated graphically: "My father's house was full of female slaves, all objects of his lust;

---

40. Beckles and Shepherd, *Liberties Lost*, 42; Keegan and Hofman, *Caribbean before Columbus*, 255.

amongst whom he strutted like Solomon in his grand seraglio, or like a bantam cock upon his own dunghill. . . . by him my mother [Rosanna] was made the object of his brutal lust."[41]

The conquest, colonization and enslavement provide tangible evidence of Europe's actions in the Caribbean that helps to support the case for reparatory justice.

## The Biblical Case

Reparatory justice also has a biblical basis. In the Book of Exodus, Moses, the great lawgiver, outlined some principles of restorative justice by way of detailed laws, including those acts of repair to be meted out to enslaved people by their enslavers. Jamaican pastor-historian the Reverend Devon Dick argues that the people of African ancestry identified their condition in slavery with that of the children of Israel; they believed that they were the new Israel and that God should treat them in the same manner as he treated the enslaved Israelites.[42] For Dick, the Judaeo-Christian faith makes allowance for reparation for gross violations against humanity, as in Deuteronomy 15:12–13: "If any of your people – Hebrew men or women – sell themselves to you and serve you six years, in the seventh year you must let them go free. And when you release them, do not send them away empty-handed." Furthermore, Exodus 3:21–22 and Exodus 11:2 state that the enslaved should not leave empty-handed but should ask for silver and gold. In other words, the enslaved should never be set free without compensation.

---

41. Robert Wedderburn, *The Horrors of Slavery and other Writings by Robert Wedderburn*, ed. Iain McCalman (Princeton, NJ: Markus Wiener, 1991). See also Trevor Burnard, *Mastery, Tyranny and Desire: Thomas Thistlewood and His Slaves in the Anglo-Jamaican World* (Chapel Hill: University of North Carolina Press; Kingston: University of the West Indies Press, 2004); Douglas Hall, *In Miserable Slavery: Thomas Thistlewood in Jamaica, 1750–86* (Kingston: University of the West Indies Press, 1999).

42. Devon Dick, "God Has Done Us an Injustice: A Baptist Pastor Makes a Biblical Case for Reparations", *Jamaica Global*, 26 July 2019, https://www.jamaica globalonline.com/god-has-done-us-an-injustice-a-baptist-pastor-makes-a-biblical-case-for-reparations/.

At the core of the biblical basis for reparation is the call for justice, which demands a bias towards those who are disadvantaged by the powerful. Justice, then, requires the intentional transformation of an existing situation of handicaps, lopsidedness and disadvantages so that the exploited can have access to facilities, opportunities, resources, goods and services for a life of real human dignity. Justice should also lead to the vindication of victims; hence reparation is about vindication for those who were victims and not compensated. Reparation for Caribbean people is about the remedy for the outrageous wrongs of slavery and indentureship and it seeks a reasonable, effective and prompt recompense through available and appropriate processes. Reparation is about more than money; it is not intended to be a monetary giveaway or a financial bonus. Reparation involves an apology but is also more than an apology; it involves restoring dignity and recognizing the immeasurable worth of each person. It seeks closure to the indignities, the discrimination, the cultural genocide, the spiritual excommunication, the rape and the killings in order to facilitate reconciliation.

The issue for Dick is not whether the Bible supports reparation but whether the Bible would support a call for reparation in the case of chattel slavery executed by Europeans. Based on the brutality of chattel slavery and the unparalleled wealth garnered over the long life of the system, there is no question that African enslavement does fit the biblical warrant for reparation.

### The Legal Case

The Caribbean's case for reparation is firmly located within a framework of law and justice; international law lays out a clear trail by linking the crime and reparation demanded for the crime. The concept of attaining justice for historic wrongs and a corresponding reparatory action has been defined by the Permanent Court of International Justice, which is today known as the International Court of Justice. The underlying principle within international law is that redress for human injustices, including crimes against humanity, is possible as long as specific conditions are met. What are these conditions, and do they exist in the case of the countries of the Caribbean, thus providing the basis for a meritorious claim for reparation?

## Conditions for a Meritorious Claim

Four basic conditions have been identified and accepted for a claim for reparation to be considered to have merit:

1. **The victims must be identifiable as a distinct group**: The Indigenous Peoples of the Caribbean who survived the harsh policies of the European countries, the descendants of enslaved Africans and people of Asian descent whose ancestors were subjected to deceptive indentureship constitute identifiable communities. The case for Indigenous Peoples and enslaved Africans is even more pressing. No other group in human history was enslaved as chattel in the same manner as black people.

2. **A defendant or defendants must exist**: In the previous chapter, we identified and provided incontrovertible evidence of those European countries that were heavily involved in indigenous genocide, human trafficking, chattel enslavement and deceptive indentureship, which led to the enrichment of their societies. The labour and output of these groups contributed to the enrichment of European societies.

3. **The injustice must be well documented**: Scholars worldwide have presented evidence of the treatment of Indigenous Peoples post-conquest, the brutal nature of the TTA and the demographic disaster caused by plantation slavery. In the case of Indigenous Peoples, one just has to read the accounts provided by scholars such as Alfred Crosby and Francisco Morales Padrón to understand the impact of European conquest (especially the Spanish, French, English and Portuguese) on their economy, society and population.[43] In the case of Africans, reference has already been

---

43. Alfred Crosby, *The Columbian Exchange: Biological and Cultural Consequences of 1492* (1972; repr., Westport, CT: Greenwood, 2003); Francisco Morales Padrón, *Spanish Jamaica*, trans. Patrick E. Bryan, Michael J. Gronow, Felix Oviedo Moral (Kingston: Ian Randle, 2003).

made to the Slave Voyages Database 2.0, which provides stark statistics on the number of Africans who embarked and those offloaded in the Americas. Of those who survived the capture and transportation under inhuman conditions and made it to the plantations of the British Caribbean, fewer than 25 per cent, or 800,000, were survivors at the time of Emancipation.

4. **The descendants of victimized groups continue to suffer harm:** The descendants of the Indigenous Peoples of the Caribbean and enslaved Africans experience a post-conquest and a post-slavery system that focuses on their race and ethnicity. The systems of wealth distribution, political marginalization and social exclusion shape their lives even today. In contrast, the rewards of the crime continue to be massive in terms of the enrichment of the descendants of the perpetrators.

## Precedents

Lord Anthony Gifford attests to the right to reparation as being well recognized in international law. He points out that the claim by peoples of the Caribbean for reparation is neither unique nor unprecedented. Indeed, the two most notorious cases of reparation occurred in the Caribbean. The first was the act by France, aided by Britain and the United States, of extracting reparations from Haiti in 1825, which has left a blight on that country up to the present. The second was at the time of Emancipation in the British-colonized Caribbean, when enslavers were paid £20 million by the British government to compensate them for the loss of their "human property". In addition, they benefited from compensation in the form of free labour under the apprenticeship system, which was negotiated as part of the compensation settlement.

### Haiti/Ayiti Pays Reparations to France

After a long and arduous ten-year war against France, the Republic of Ayiti declared its independence in 1804. A 500,000-strong nation, Ayiti declared that any person of African descent who entered its borders would be declared a free citizen of its republic. The French, however, declared Haiti an illegal pariah state, refusing to acknowledge its independence as legitimate. Other countries from the West shared this stance with France, including the United States, which the Haitians had hoped would stand in solidarity with them. As a result, Haiti was isolated and denied access to world trade and development.

By 1825, as the republic celebrated its twenty-first anniversary, the Haitian economy was suffering from bankruptcy due to its isolation. Recognizing that this could not continue, the Haitian government invited its former French colonizers to a summit. The French expressed willingness to recognize Haiti as a state only if Haiti would pay reparations to the French of 150 million francs. This sum was based on the French valuation of land, services, commercial properties, physical assets and the formerly enslaved Haitian people (including members of the Haitian cabinet). With little that could be done, Haiti agreed. Haiti began payments immediately and was forced to pay a total of 90 million francs, up until 1947, when the last instalment was paid. With payments made to France amounting to up to 70 per cent of Haiti's foreign exchange earnings, the country's economy was bled dry and, as a result of this blatant exploitation, Haiti was termed a failed state. It is this blatant exploitation that led to the destruction of the Republic of Haiti.

In 2004, Haiti's then president Jean-Bertrand Aristide made a formal request to France for the restitution of US$21 billion, equivalent to the 90 million gold francs it forcibly extracted from Haiti. His request was met with hostility, however, as the Americans invaded Haiti and Aristide was forced to flee his country. Even though activists continued to call for restitution, the fact that the formal demand by Aristide was rescinded by succeeding governments has affected Haiti's reparation. Aristide's request was, however, the first time that a postcolonial Caribbean government had made an official request for reparation to a European government.[44]

---

44. Beckles, "Hate and the Quake".

## German Payment to Jews

The most often cited case is that of the state of Germany as well as individual German firms, which began in 1952 paying the state of Israel and individual survivors of the Jewish Holocaust reparations each year. By 2014, the total paid was more than €120 million. Much later, in 1990, Austria also made payments of US$25 million to survivors of the Jewish Holocaust. Gifford argues that there is no legal barrier to prevent those who still suffer the consequences of crimes against humanity from claiming reparations, even though the crimes were committed against their ancestors. He adds that claims have been made not only by descendants, but also by the nation state that has had to bear the burden of paying for the consequences of the crime. He cites the case of Israel, which successfully claimed reparations from West Germany for the costs of resettling Jewish refugees even though the state of Israel did not exist at the time when the Nazi regime committed the crimes against the Jews. It is also significant that West Germany, which felt obliged to meet the claim, was also a different state territorially and politically from the German Reich, which was responsible for the atrocities.

## US Government Payment to the Japanese

There is a second category where a state has accepted the responsibility to make restitution to groups of people within its own borders where rights have been violated. Between 1942 and 1946, Japanese Americans were interned in large numbers as a result of the attack on the United States by imperial Japan during World War II. In 1988, the US Congress passed the Civil Liberties Act, which was designed to make restitution to Japanese Americans in respect of losses brought about by any discriminatory act by the US government based on the individual's Japanese ancestry during the wartime period. A total of US$1.2 billion was paid, in addition to a formal apology and restitution to those individuals of Japanese ancestry.

## *Apology and Payment to Maori People*

In 1995, Queen Elizabeth II added her signature, as head of state of New Zealand, to the apology addressed to the Maori people in New Zealand who were massacred and whose lands were seized in the 1860s, under the rulership of her ancestor Queen Victoria. As the queen of New Zealand, Queen Elizabeth gave royal assent to the act of Parliament which outlined the compensation of the Tainui people for the brutality and suffering they endured in the 1860s.[45]

## *Apology and Payment to the Mau Mau*

In 2013, a settlement of £20 million was paid to Kenyans who endured torture by British colonial forces as a result of their fight for freedom in the Mau Mau protest in the 1950s. Then British foreign secretary William Hague announced that the government of the United Kingdom "sincerely regrets" the abuse inflicted on Kenyan people, but he stopped short of an outright apology and the settlement did not include those who died, in keeping with the stance of the British government towards reparation.[46]

Other precedents for reparation that are often cited include the following:

- In 2008, then Canadian prime minister Stephen Harper issued an apology to the aboriginal peoples of Canada for the "Indian Residential Schools" policy, acknowledging that it had a damaging impact on their culture, heritage and language.

---

45. David Barber Wellington, "The Queen Says Sorry to Wronged Maoris", *Independent*, 2 November 1995, https://www.independent.co.uk/news/world/the-queen-says-sorry-to-wronged-maoris-1536901.html.
46. "Mau Mau Torture Victims to Receive Compensation – Hague", *BBC News*, 6 June 2013, https://www.bbc.com/news/uk-22790037.

- In 2008, the Australian government apologized for its treatment of indigenous Australian peoples after an official enquiry labelled it genocide.
- In 2009, the Obama administration agreed to pay US$1.4 billion to a group of Native Americans who claimed the government mismanaged a century-old system of land trusts.
- In 2011, then prime minister Tony Blair apologized to the Irish for Britain's role in the potato famine of the nineteenth century.

The precedents across the globe for reparation are summarized in table 3.1 (page 59).

## Reparation and Apologies within the Caribbean

Closer to home, in 2017, Jamaica's prime minister Andrew Holness issued an apology to the Rastafari community for the atrocities committed against its members in the 1963 Coral Gardens massacre, less than a year after Jamaican independence, during the prime ministership of Alexander Bustamante. A relatively minor land dispute involving one member of the Rastafari community led to violence, which elicited a massive state crackdown against the Rastafari community, which resulted in three deaths, the mass rounding up and arrest of over 150 brethren, and general discrimination against Rastafari men and women. Holness, fifty-four years later, acknowledged that an injustice had been perpetrated against the Rastafari and announced the setting up of a trust fund of J$10 million (approximately US$80,000 at that time) to assist the beneficiaries of those who suffered loss during the incident. Subsequently, activism by Rastafari has led to the increase of this fund to approximately US$99,000.

In 2018, Antigua and Barbuda's prime minister Gaston Browne followed suit by issuing an apology to the Rastafari community for the police brutality and castigation inflicted upon them for the use of cannabis, an integral element to their spiritual practices. Browne, in his address on World Cannabis Day, said, "Let us regard this as reparations for Rastafari, for the wrongs inflicted on this

Table 3.1. A sample of reparation settlements

| Date | Paid by | Paid to | Amount | Notes |
|---|---|---|---|---|
| 1825 | Haiti | France: "slave-owner reparations" | 150 million gold francs | Haiti had to borrow first instalment from French bank; amount reduced to 90 million francs; paid this off by 1947 |
| 1834 | Britain | "Slave-owner reparations" | £20 million | Jamaican planters received more than £6 million (or one third of the total) |
| 1952 | Germany | Israel, World Jewish Congress | $65.2 billion | For atrocities committed during the Holocaust and for the resettlement of Jews |
| 1988 | United States | Japanese-Americans | $1.2 billion | Payments of $20,000 each to Japanese Americans interned in camps during World War II |
| 1995 | Government of New Zealand | Maoris | $170 million | Money paid in compensation for the theft of land by settlers in 1863 |
| 2008 | Italy | Libya | $5 billon | Italy's colonial occupation of Libya |
| 2009 | United States (Obama Administration) | Native Americans | $1.4 billion | Land claim; to a group of Native Americans who said the government mismanaged a century-old system of Indian land trusts |
| 2012 | Britain | Mau Mau, Kenya | £19.9 million | For colonial atrocities committed against the Mau Mau in their fight for liberation |
| July 2013 | Japan | South Koreans | £230,000 | For forced labour during Japan's colonization of Korea |

*Source*: Jamaica National Reparation Commission, "Report on the Work of the National Commission on Reparations, May 2009–October 2013", 33.

significant minority group in our countries through the so-called 'war on drugs' which evidently was prompted by pernicious prohibition."[47]

## Summary of the Legal Case

1. **Enslavement was and is a crime against humanity**: African enslavement and the TTA were crimes against humanity, defined as including murder, extermination, enslavement, deportation and other inhuman acts against any civilian population. There is an abundance of historical evidence to demonstrate that enslavement of Africans was a form of genocide and that the indigenous people of the Caribbean suffered genocide at the hands of the Europeans.

2. **The right to reparation is recognized in international law**: Those who commit crimes against humanity must make reparation.

3. **There is no legal barrier** to prevent those who still suffer the consequences of enslavement from claiming reparation even though the crimes were committed against their ancestors.

## The Consequences and Legacies of Slavery and Colonialism

### Psychological

In the British-colonized Caribbean, colonialism, slavery and other forms of unfree labour gave rise to poverty, landlessness and underdevelopment as well as to the destruction of cultures and languages, the loss of identity, and the inculcation of inferiority among the descendants of those affected by these systems of oppression. The indoctrination of "white" into a racist mindset continues to affect the prospects and quality of lives of African and Indigenous Peoples in the Caribbean.

---

47. "Antigua Apologises to Rastafari Community", *Jamaica Observer*, 19 April 2018, http://www.jamaicaobserver.com/news/antigua-apologises-to-rastafari-community_130892.

## Failure to Repatriate

With a conservative estimate of over 15 million Africans kidnapped from their homes and forcibly transported to the Caribbean (not to mention those who died in the process of capture and shipment), the TTA is the largest forced migration in human history. Many people of African descent in the region have long experienced a feeling of displacement and loss of identity as they still grapple with the difficulties of identifying with a location that is not their true home. There is, therefore, need for a repatriation programme, for those who desire it, to allow resettlement on the African continent.

## Health

With respect to health, it is conservatively estimated that 70 per cent of people of the region over the age of fifty suffer from hypertension and diabetes, or both, because of the high salt and sugar content of the slavery diet. As a community of people addicted to salt and sugar, many Caribbean people now cannot metabolize either, hence the prevalence of hypertension and diabetes.

> For three hundred years every single day morning, noon and night we're eating sugar and salt – the only people in the world consigned to that fate. I know this because walking to primary school, barefooted, our grandmother would give us a little half a pound bag of sugar and when you were hungry you ate sugar as a meal. But that was the nature of all the poor people on the island. And now Barbados is called the amputation capital of the world because there is more amputation of limbs of black people in Barbados per capita anywhere in the world and why? Because Barbados was an island of pure sugar production, 80% of the land space of Barbados was sugar and the people ate sugar morning, noon and night.[48]

---

48. Hilary McD. Beckles, "Relinquishing Doubt and Moving Forward in the Context of Reparations", *Jamaica Global*, 27 July 2019, https://www.jamaicaglobalonline.com/is-reparations-really-an-impossible-dream-what-you-always-thought-you-knew-but-didnt/.

## Colonialism and Neo-Colonialism

The period of conquest, which so affected the Indigenous Peoples of the Caribbean, the forced relocation of Africans, the introduction of chattel slavery and later other forms of bonded labour were all features of colonialism. It is now generally accepted that colonialism itself can be considered a crime against humanity in international law, for it was a usurpation imposed by force on the right of colonized peoples to their sovereignty. Until independence, Caribbean people had no voice or status in the international community: their countries were considered overseas possessions of the very country whose people had kidnapped and enslaved their ancestors.

# 4

# The Strategy
## The CARICOM Ten-Point Plan

The Caribbean reparation movement has gained momentum and achieved legitimacy through the public alignment and practical support of the heads of government of the Caribbean through CARICOM. At the thirty-fourth meeting of the Conference of Heads of Government, in July 2013, it was decided to set up national committees on reparation in each CARICOM state to establish the moral, ethical and legal case for payment of reparation by the former colonial European countries, to the nations and peoples of the Caribbean Community, for native genocide, the transatlantic trafficking in Africans, a racialized system of chattel enslavement and continuing harm through the legacies of slavery.[49]

Reparation for deceptive Asian indentureship has also been included, based on the many violations, poor treatment and unfilled contractual terms of the indentureship system.

To date, several reparation committees have been formed across the Caribbean, with members drawn from a wide cross-section of Caribbean society. In addition, they have established links with reparation activists and networks from Canada to Curaçao and

---

49. CARICOM Reparations Commission, https://caricomreparations.org/.

from Brazil to Belgium. The countries in which national committees have been formed are Antigua and Barbuda, the Bahamas, Barbados, Dominica, Grenada, Guyana, Jamaica, St Kitts and Nevis, St Lucia, St Vincent and the Grenadines, Suriname, and Trinidad and Tobago. Reparation advocates continue to work across the region, even where no formal committee has been established or re-established.

The Conference of Heads of Government agreed at its Thirty-Fourth Regular Meeting, held in 2013 in Trinidad and Tobago, to establish a CARICOM Reparations Commission comprising the chairpersons of the national committees and a representative of the University of the West Indies. The CRC reports to the Prime Ministerial Sub-Committee on Reparations, which is chaired by the prime minister of Barbados. They also requested the establishment of the Centre for Reparation Research as the research and educational arm of the CRC. The centre was officially launched in 2017. One of the first outputs of the CRC was the Ten-Point Action Plan, which was accepted by CARICOM Heads of Government.[50] The plan outlines the path to truth, justice and reconciliation and provides the basis for negotiations for reparation with former colonial powers, including Denmark, France, the Netherlands, Spain, Portugal, and the United Kingdom. Other countries that may be identified through further research or their own admission of guilt will be added. As we have seen in chapter 2, Germany, Norway and Sweden may be identified as lesser-known active participants in the TTA.

The rationale for the plan can be summarized as follows:

- European governments invaded and captured the lands of the region that were occupied by Caribbean civilizations.
- These governments facilitated genocidal actions against Indigenous communities. As the Indigenous populations declined in numbers owing to atrocities committed against them, Europeans, with the participation of their governments, began capturing and transporting Africans to the Caribbean.

---

50. For more details, email reparation.research@uwimona.edu.jm, the Centre for Reparation Research.

- Europeans became owners and traders of enslaved Africans and defined and enforced African enslavement and native genocide as being in their national interests. At the same time, their governments created the legal and financial policies necessary for the enslavement of Africans.

Through their agents (that is, enslavers/plantation owners), European governments imposed a system of terror on Africans through the plantation system. For several decades, they opposed efforts to end the African holocaust and severely punished Africans who resisted.

When finally forced to abandon the illegal trade in enslaved Africans and the system of enslavement, European governments refused compensation to the enslaved while compensating the enslavers. They imposed a further hundred years of racial apartheid upon the emancipated people.

European governments have steadfastly refused to acknowledge such crimes or to compensate victims and their descendants, who continue to suffer harm and the legacies of colonialism.

## The CARICOM Ten-Point Plan for Reparatory Justice and Its Rationale

### 1. A Full and Formal Apology

The descendants of the Indigenous Peoples subjected to genocide, the loss of several cultures and the erasure of numerous languages require a full and formal apology. The descendants of the enslaved African population subjected to deadly forced migration and a system of colonialism that destroyed their bodies and their cultures require a full and formal apology. Groups subjected to deceptive systems of indenture deserve a full and formal apology. All the ancestors who were destroyed or affected by colonialism, their descendants alive today and future generations require a full and formal apology. Only a full and formal apology can allow for the healing of wounds, including the destruction of cultures caused by colonialism (enslavement and other forms of oppression of peoples). A full apology accepts responsibility, commits to non-repetition and pledges to repair the harm done. Governments from countries responsible for the destruction have refused to offer apologies and have instead issued "statements of regret". These statements do not acknowledge that crimes have been committed and they represent a refusal to take responsibility.

## 2. Indigenous Peoples Development Programmes

As a result of European conquest and colonization, the Indigenous Peoples within the member states of CARICOM have been subjected to forced migration within countries and across the region, to brutal work conditions, and to genocide. Indigenous Peoples were brutalized and killed as a result of official instructions to the European military commanders who came to the region. Those who were not immediately killed had their ancestral lands seized. A community of 3 million people in 1700 was reduced to fewer than 30,000 in 2000, their language and unique cultural heritage destroyed. The descendants of Indigenous Peoples remain traumatized and landless, and they are one of the most marginalized groups in the region as a result of the deliberate and racist discrimination on the part of the European colonizers.

Despite the efforts of the newly developing CARICOM member states that have inherited the situation, the rebuilding of these communities cannot be done without responsible European states correcting the damage they did and, where possible, restoring the communities that still exist.

## 3. Funding for Repatriation to Africa

The descendants of African peoples stolen from their homes, lands, people and cultures have a legal right of return. Unlike indentured workers, the enslaved had no contract guaranteeing the right to return or material incentives to remain. It is the duty of those states that are responsible for the forced movement and enslavement of their ancestors to establish a resettlement programme for those who wish to return. CARICOM has already been in contact with African states that are willing and able to allow for the return of their stolen people. However, the burden of funding the resettlement of those who had been moved as a result of crimes by European states cannot be borne by the victims of the crimes. A fully funded resettlement programme that allows for the repatriation of the displaced Africans in CARICOM member states who wish to return, while also addressing such issues as citizenship and reintegration, is crucial to correcting the wrongs of enslavement and colonialism.

### 4. The Establishment of Cultural Institutions and the Return of Cultural Heritage

Part of the devastation of European colonization was the deliberate attempt to destroy the cultures and languages of the Indigenous Peoples, enslaved Africans and indentured workers. Generations later, this devastation has left a gap in the knowledge of some of these groups about the history of their ancestors and an inability to deeply comprehend the full lives and cultures they had before European colonization, the trauma they endured during the process, how they eventually gained freedom, and the strides they are taking slowly to rebuild.

The restoration of historical memory through community institutions, such as museums and research centres, will allow citizens to understand these crimes against humanity as well as other colonial harm and to memorialize their ancestors' contributions to modern disciplines, such as health care and technology. The absence of these institutions contributes to a sense of rootlessness of these groups within the region. The return of looted items by colonialists and the display of these and other cultural heritage artefacts in the region would also allow Caribbean schoolteachers, children and academic researchers to have access to the information that is now locked almost exclusively within European institutions.

Though some private institutions have been established, CARICOM member states have not been able, with their extremely limited resources, to build these institutions on their own. The

Caribbean Reparatory Justice Programme maintains that the destruction of historical memory is a crime for which reparation must be made.

## 5. Remedying the Public Health Crisis

CARICOM member states are committed to providing high standards of health care for their populations, in accordance with their international obligations. On their own, however, they are unable to deal with the multiple diseases that affect the majority of their populations and are the legacy of enslavement.

For example, the African-descended population in the Caribbean is among those with a high incidence of chronic diseases in the form of hypertension and type 2 diabetes. New medical evidence has shown that these diseases are a result of the nutritional experience, physical and emotional brutality and overall stress profiles associated with four hundred years of enslavement. The centuries of poor nutrition and overly salted foods given to the enslaved have now transmitted an intergenerational tendency to hypertension. This has devastating consequences for a health-care system that was deliberately made inadequate by European colonizers and is now slowly being built by CARICOM member states. The public health crisis is a burden that these states cannot shoulder on their own: these chronic health conditions now constitute the greatest financial risk to sustainability in the region.

Dealing with this health crisis requires the injection of science, technology and capital beyond the capacity of the region. European countries that are responsible for the crisis have an obligation to participate in its alleviation and to restore good health through the provision of hospitals and health care.

## 6. Education Programmes

There was barely an attempt during the period of enslavement and colonialism to establish a proper education system to serve the needs of Indigenous Peoples, enslaved Africans and indentured workers. This unwillingness may be attributed to the deliberate desire of colonizers to have an uneducated labour force dedicated to back-breaking and deadly work.

At the end of European colonialism, the black, indigenous and indentured communities in CARICOM member states were left in a general state of illiteracy. Where an education system did exist, it tended to be European-influenced and based on race and class inequality.

CARICOM governments inherited a flawed education system, inadequate schools, high illiteracy rates and a system founded on structural discrimination. Although they have worked hard to correct the situation, widespread functional illiteracy and inequitable systems of education still exist. This flawed education system has subverted the development efforts of these states and represents a drag upon social and economic advancement.

European states that presided over this system of inequality have a responsibility to build on the laudable efforts of the CARICOM postcolonial regimes, expand educational capacity and provide scholarships. Development requires a highly educated population.

7. **Enhancement of Historical and Cultural Knowledge Exchanges**

Colonialism created the situation where European culture was forced on the Indigenous Peoples of the region, those who were forcibly brought to the region and those who were brought under partially voluntary contracts. This forced acculturation was based on the racist idea that the full and rich cultures of each of these groups were "inferior" and needed to be erased. European colonizers intentionally distanced people from the sources of their culture and belonging.

There was a particularly deliberate effort on the part of responsible European countries to destroy African heritage. Other groups brought to the CARICOM region had a right to return to their homeland and learn about their history and peoples, but there was no general right to return for enslaved Africans. This policy of deliberate disconnection was part and parcel of the colonial project. Forced separation of Africans from their homeland has resulted in cultural and social alienation from identity and existential belonging.

The forced migration of Indigenous Peoples to various places and countries throughout the region, as well as their mass destruction through genocide, has also led to a sense of rootlessness among them.

CARICOM member states have spent the last fifty years trying to reverse the impact of centuries of disconnection. Part of reparatory justice therefore requires a programme of restoration of pride, and one way of doing this is to intensify efforts to rebuild "bridges of belonging". The region cannot do it alone. The years of creating this programme represent an undue burden on newly developing states that must tackle other development challenges.

School exchanges and culture tours, community artistic and performance programmes, entrepreneurial and religious engagements, as well as political interaction, are required in order to fill the void created by slave voyages and the forced destruction of the history and culture of indigenous and indentured groups.

CARICOM has made important advances in developing connections with the homelands in Africa, the Caribbean and Asia to facilitate cultural exchanges. Nevertheless, expanding funding of these programmes is part of repairing the destruction of colonization and must be borne by responsible European states.

## 8. Psychological Rehabilitation as a Result of the Transmission of Trauma

The history of colonialism by certain European states has inflicted serious psychological trauma upon indigenous and African-descendant populations. African and Indigenous Peoples therefore need rehabilitation for their affected populations. Mental health issues need to be treated like physical manifestations of illness.

Medical evidence from other traumatized populations now demonstrates that there can be intergenerational transmission of trauma. It is plausible to argue that Africans have experienced intergenerational trauma from colonization, the Middle Passage, enslavement, terror and brutalization and genocide, and that this is in the DNA of the descendants of the survivors.

Though CARICOM member states have attempted to provide rehabilitation support for the massive incidences of psychological trauma, the scarce resources and development challenges have meant that mental health care has lagged behind. Responsible European states have an obligation to repair the psychological trauma caused by colonialism and its evils in order to assist in rebuilding full and whole men, women and children.

### 9. The Right to Development through the Use of Technology

For four hundred years, the trade and production policies of Europe could be summed up in the British slogan "Not a nail is to be made in the colonies".[51] This was a deliberate decision to retard the technology available for development within CARICOM member states.

The effectiveness of this policy meant that CARICOM member states entered their nation-building phases technologically and scientifically ill-equipped to participate in the postmodern world economy.

Generations of youth within the region, as a consequence, have been denied access to the science and technology culture and this represents an undue burden on the development of these states. Technology transfer and science-sharing for development by responsible European states are important parts of repairing the deliberate harm to the development prospects of countries within CARICOM.

### 10. Debt Cancellation and Monetary Compensation

CARICOM governments that emerged from slavery and colonialism have inherited the massive crisis of community poverty and an inability to deal with the development of their countries because of the legacy of colonialism. Since correcting this legacy has fallen on

---

51. Hilary McDonald Beckles, "White Labour in Black Slave Plantation Society and Economy: A Case Study of Indentured Labour in Seventeenth Century Barbados" (PhD diss., University of Hull, 1980), 271.

these new states, they have been forced to take on onerous levels of debt in order to meet their own international obligations.

CARICOM member states recognize the importance of providing the highest standards of living for their citizens. The pressure of development has driven these governments to carry the burden of public employment and has led them to create expensive social policies designed to confront colonial legacies. This process has resulted in states accumulating unsustainable levels of public debt that now constitutes "fiscal entrapment".

This debt cycle properly belongs to the governments of the responsible European countries, but they have made no sustained attempt to deal with debilitating colonial legacies. Support for the payment of domestic debt, the cancellation of international debt and direct monetary payments, where appropriate, are necessary reparatory actions to correct the harm caused by colonialism.

Although the overall intention of the plan is to negotiate a development package, at the very least, Britain and other nations that paid compensation to enslavers should return the sums paid in current values.

## The Use of the Plan

The Ten-Point Plan is intended to be used as a public education tool as well as the basis for negotiation with former colonizers for reparatory justice for the people of the region.

# 5

# No Apology, No Reparation
## Europe's Stance

The first requirement of the CARICOM Ten-Point Plan is for the guilty nations of Europe to apologize for the crimes they have committed against Caribbean people. As discussed in chapter 3, but relevant to this chapter also, apology has three components:

1. Acknowledgement that a wrong has been committed
2. Commitment to non-repetition
3. Willingness to make amends

An apology differs from a statement of "regret" or "remorse", because neither one of those accepts responsibility for the consequences of one's action. As the reparation movement has gained traction in the twenty-first century, a number of European states, as well as leading figures in their governments, have issued statements of regret. Notable among them was the Dutch government, which at the Durban Conference in 2001 expressed "remorse" but offered no apologies that would have meant accepting responsibility for the legacy of the crime. From the British side, former prime ministers Tony Blair and David Cameron have both issued statements of regret, in 2007 and 2015 respectively,[52] but have stopped short of facilitating any engagement of discussion on reparation. As a legal admission of guilt, an apology would by definition call for restitution and rehabilitation, compensation, satisfaction and a guarantee of non-repetition for the victims and their descendants.[53] This may include monetary compensation, memorialization, institutional and educational reforms, the return of stolen cultural property, and other forms of redress, as outlined in the Ten-Point Plan. By refusing to issue an apology, European states hope to be legally protected from responsibility for repairing the damage done by slavery.

All approaches to guilty European nations have been met with denial and refusal even to discuss the question of reparation. Instead, they have sought to mount a rigid defence, which has been systematically and successfully challenged by advocates of reparation. In examining the arguments put forward against reparation, our analysis will focus on the attitude and response of the British in relation to the British-colonized Caribbean, since they were the main beneficiary of the profits from selling enchained Africans and built their fortune and power from the sweat and blood of millions of oppressed people. We will examine the following three arguments advanced by apologists for and supporters of the British government and the government itself:

1. Chattel enslavement was legal at the time.
2. Africans were complicit in the operations of the transatlantic trade and the enslavement of fellow Africans.
3. The people who have suffered the injustice are all dead, so why should the descendants of the perpetrators be responsible for the sins of their ancestors? This argument was most recently

---

52. "Blair Says 'Sorry' for Slavery", *Reuters*, 20 March 2007, https://www.reuters.com/article/us-britain-blair-slavery-idUSMOL06003620070320; "David Cameron Rules out Slavery Reparation during Jamaica Visit", *BBC*, 30 September 2015, https://www.bbc.com/news/uk-34401412.

53. See "Report of the United Nations Special Rapporteur on Contemporary Forms of Racism, Racial Discrimination, Xenophobia and Racial Intolerance", UN General Assembly (A/74/321), 21 August 2019, https://www.ohchr.org/Documents/Issues/Racism/SR/A_74_231_Reparations_%20SR%20Racism.pdf.

articulated in 2021 by then UK high commissioner to Jamaica Asif Ahmad. Ahmad dismissed the nation's claim for reparation after Jamaica announced its intention to file a petition to seek compensation from Britain for its participation in the transatlantic trade in Africans. Ahmad said that the request for reparation directly from government to government "will not prosper" because it would be difficult to know who to make the payment to as those directly harmed by the activity "are no longer here".[54]

## "Chattel enslavement was legal at the time": Argument and Rejoinders

The British government has argued that there was no genocide practised against the native Caribbean population and that black enslavement was not a criminal action. During the period of colonial rule, some of their citizens in the region defined natives as "savages" and classified Africans as chattel or property. They argue that chattel enslavement of Africans was legal at the time since it was sanctioned by the imperial government, which was acting within the context of "acceptable" European norms. All other European governments were involved in slavery and this made it an international standard not considered criminal at the time it was enforced. An allied argument was that even if chattel enslavement was indeed a crime, those crimes are now too remote and not subject to political recuperation.

Caribbean citizens beg to differ, as the rejoinders that follow will illustrate.

### Rejoinder 1

With respect to the claim of "remoteness", legally, there is no statute of limitation on a guilty party or state's making restitution for crimes against humanity. It is also an acceptable response to point out that the descendants of victims of the crimes of chattel slavery continue

---

54. Edmond Campbell, "Simply Not Happening", *Gleaner*, 20 July 2021, https://jamaica-gleaner.com/article/lead-stories/20210720/simply-not-happening.

to bear not only the memory of what was done to their ancestors, but also the consequences of the crime in the state of underdevelopment that bedevils the nations of the Caribbean.

## Rejoinder 2

The early modern world witnessed various forms of slavery and servitude as systems of labour, but neither in Europe nor in Africa did this subservience involve the branding of people as chattel. Chattel slavery developed in the Caribbean as a special and specific European practice that targeted Africans. No other racial or ethnic group that entered the English-colonized Caribbean received this legal classification. *By defining Africans as legal non-humans, perpetual property and reproductive chattels, the British are guilty of introducing racism to the Caribbean, the Americas and the Western world in general.*

## Rejoinder 3

The legal argument that there was no crime in enslaving black people since all white people were doing it and it was a common activity for European colonizers does not stand up to the strict scrutiny of British law. It is also insufficient to argue that chattel slavery was legalized by the colonial governments, because we know that colonial laws were sanctioned by the British government in London. It is also a historical fact that the highest courts in England held that chattel slavery was incompatible with English law. In the famous Somerset judgment of 1772, Lord Mansfield, the chief justice, held that slavery had no basis in common law and had never been established by legislation in England and therefore was not binding in law. In the *Knight vs Wedderburn* case in Scotland, the judge was even more explicit, declaring that "the state of slavery is not recognized by the laws of this Kingdom . . . the laws of Jamaica being unjust could not be supported in this country".[55]

---

55. Jermaine O. McCalpin, "Summary of the Arguments for and against Reparation for Slavery: Point-Counterpoint", in *Jamaica and the Debate over Reparation for Slavery: A Discussion Paper*, ed. Verene Shepherd, Ahmed Reid,

Further, during the Reparations Under International Law Symposium organized by the American Society of International Law in May 2021, leading scholars of international law demonstrated that chattel slavery was illegal by the laws of African nations at the time, many of which strongly resisted the heinous trade of European traffickers, and was also illegal in several European countries, including Spain, Portugal and the United Kingdom. There was no provision for the trade in enslaved Africans in any conventions or legal instruments at the time and customary international law did not uphold slavery and the trade in enslaved Africans.[56]

### "Africans were complicit in the operations of the transatlantic trade and the enslavement of fellow Africans": Argument and Rejoinder

The argument is that the TTA and slavery in the Americas were merely an extension of the existing trade in enslaved Africans and slavery in Africa, which had been going on for centuries and that there was nothing new in what the Europeans were doing in their colonies.

### Rejoinder

This is a misconception that can be rebutted on several levels:

- The major difference between European-introduced TTA and slavery and precolonial slavery in Africa is that, in the former, humans were treated as the property of other humans and forced to produce labour.
- Precolonial slavery was based on incidental war and debt while the TTA was based on systematic hunt and capture.
- The TTA was an industry that became part of the rise of the global economy. Precolonial slavery was regionally limited.

---

Cavell Francis and Kameika Murphy (Kingston: Pelican, 2012), appendix 4, 95–97.

56. See also Nora Wittman, "An International Law Deconstruction of the Hegemonic Denial of the Right to Reparations", *Social and Economic Studies* 68, nos. 3–4 (2019): 19–41; Anthony Gifford, "Key Legal Aspects of the Claim for Reparation", *Social and Economic Studies* 68, nos. 3–4 (2019): 249–52.

- The TTA linked interests on multiple continents and became an integral part of an industrial infrastructure that linked human trafficking to other economic activities, such as finance, shipping, the food and clothing industries, and manufacturing in Europe and North America.
- The European system of capture was conceptualized and executed as a business of private entrepreneurs that was sanctioned by states. In precolonial Africa, such capitalist business was absent.
- The ideology of racism and the practice of institutional racism were developed, expanded and became entrenched across Europe and the Americas.
- The argument that Africans sold each other to Europeans seeks to shift the responsibility for slavery from the Europeans to Africans. It also fails to recognize that the idea of a shared African identity did not exist when Europeans began to capture Africans to transport them to the Americas. Ethnic groups in Africa were divided by language, religion and other cultural traits, and some were long-term adversaries. Europeans played on these divisions, often using force as well as trade, especially in weapons, and sometimes bribery. Groups in conflict with each other will help outside parties. African leaders who refused to cooperate with the European slavers could expect war.

It should also be noted that Africans resisted the TTA on many levels and at every stage of the TTA. The books *Trading Souls* and *Saving Souls* by Hilary Beckles and Verene Shepherd (see the bibliography), as well as data provided by the Lowcountry Digital History Initiative, indicate that Africans did not accept capture, shipping and enslavement without opposition. Africans who were enslaved or threatened with enslavement consistently resisted. Villages and towns built fortifications and warning systems to prevent attacks from traders or enemy groups. If captured and forced onto ships for the Middle Passage, enslaved Africans resisted by organizing hunger strikes, forming rebellions, and even dying by suicide by leaping overboard rather than living in slavery. Scholars believe that roughly one slaving voyage in every ten experienced major protests, which were costly for European traders and led them to avoid certain regions known for this resistance strategy, such as Upper Guinea, except during periods of high market demand. This resulted in fewer Africans entering the TTA from these regions, which suggests that African resistance strategies could be effective.

One of the earliest documented cases of resistance is the correspondence of the Kongo ruler Nzinga Mbemba (also known as Afonso I, c. 1446–1543), who wrote to the king of Portugal, João III, in 1526 to demand an end to the illegal depopulation of his kingdom. The Kongolese king's successor, Garcia II, made similar unsuccessful protests. Other African rulers took a stand as well. For instance, in the early seventeenth century, Nzinga Mbandi (c. 1583–1663), queen of Ndongo (modern-day Angola), fought against the Portuguese – part of a century-long campaign of resistance waged by the kingdom against the trade in enslaved africans. Anti-slavery motives can also be found in the activities of the Christian leader Dona Beatriz Kimpa Vita (1684–1706) in Kongo.

Several major African states took measures to limit and suppress the TTA, including the kingdoms of Benin and Dahomey. Agaja Trudo, the king of Dahomey (r. 1708–1740), banned the TTA and even went as far as attacking the European forts on the coast. In West Africa, several Muslim states were opposed to the trafficking of humans, including Futa Toro in the Senegal River basin, in the late eighteenth century, and Futa Jallon in what is now Guinea, in the early nineteenth century. In Futa Jallon, the religious leader Abd al-Qadir wrote a letter to British traders threatening death to anyone who tried to procure enslaved people in his country.

Many ordinary Africans also took measures to protect themselves from enslavement. Flight was the most obvious method, but there is also evidence that many Africans moved their villages to more inaccessible areas or took other measures to protect them. In his autobiography *The Interesting Narrative of the Life of Olaudah Equiano*, the author mentions some of the defensive measures that were taken in his own village.

Resistance continued on the Middle Passage and on plantations in the Caribbean, with major wars fought by the enslaved from the sixteenth to nineteenth centuries.

## "The people who have suffered the injustice are all dead": Argument and Rejoinder

The anti-reparationists claim that the people who suffered the injustice are all dead and therefore the descendants of the perpetrators should not be held responsible for the sins of their ancestors.

### Rejoinder

The statement and accompanying question imply that historical events of as vast reach as slavery have no material impact on the present. In fact, what happened to or was done by African ancestors filters down and has an impact on the present. In a thought-provoking article published in the *New Statesman*, Priyamvada Gopal asks: "How is it possible, at one and the same time, to believe deeply in the right to inherit wealth and property acquired by progenitors while insisting that we in the present cannot, in any way, be responsible for the mechanisms of wealth-making in the past? It's convenient enough: my grandfather's house is *my* house but how he came to own it is none of my business."[57]

Many of the people who have profited from the injustice are still alive, having inherited the wealth generated by the system of slavery. They should have a balanced inheritance, inheriting not only the wealth but also the debts of their ancestors. In chapter 2, reference was made to the findings of the Centre for the Study of the Legacies of British Slavery at University College London, which shows that many contemporary millionaires and politicians, as well as ordinary

---

57. Priyamvada Gopal, "Much of Britain's Wealth Is Built on Slavery. So Why Shouldn't It Pay Reparations?" *New Statesman*, 23 April 2014, https://www.newstatesman.com/economics/2014/04/much-britains-wealth-built-slavery-so-why-shouldnt-it-pay-reparations.

middle-class people, come from families who were compensated for the loss of property in enslaved Africans in the Caribbean. The freed Africans never received such compensation and their families inherited instead the poverty and landlessness that blight them to this day. Capitalism itself, along with the cheap beach holidays enjoyed by present-day British tourists who flock to the Caribbean, would have been impossible without slavery.

There are other examples of the ways in which current families are linked to the profits of slavery. For instance, Harewood House, seat of the Lascelles family, is one of the treasure houses of England, but its splendour masks a dark past.

The Lascelles family's rise to wealth and earldom were obtained through their participation in the TTA and slavery. In fact, Henry Lascelles, to whom the family's original wealth is often attributed, was the son of farmers. He acquired his wealth, alongside his brothers, through the importation of enslaved people from Africa to properties in Barbados and through the enslaved people's labour being used for sugar production and exportation, beginning from as early as 1648. Henry later returned to London, where he acquired a parliamentary seat and was regarded as one of England's wealthiest men. It was one of Henry's sons, Edwin, who retained control of the Harewood estate and commissioned the building of Harewood House. During this time Edwin also "added 22 more plantations in the West Indies and nearly 3,000 more slaves to his portfolio, taking advantage of the collapse in the sugar export market during the American War of Independence". In 1790, Edwin was made first Baron Harewood, commencing the family's English nobility, which continues today. In fact, it is important to note that the sixth earl of the family, Henry Lascelles, married Princess Mary, who was the daughter of King George V and the aunt of Queen Elizabeth II. When faced with information about their wealth owing to the TTA and slavery, David Lascelles had this to say: "We have to try to be positive. There's absolutely nothing we can do about the past, we can't travel back in time to change the bad things our ancestors did."[58]

---

58. Grace Newton, "How Harewood House in Yorkshire Was Built with the

The Drax family is another example of present-day families that have benefited from the wealth generated by the system of slavery. The Drax family are the current owners of the Drax Hall plantation in Barbados – a plantation which has been owned by them since the period of enslavement (1650) and was one of the scenes of the enslavement of African people in Barbados for centuries. In 2021, Conservative member of Parliament Richard Drax faced demands for the handing over of his 621-acre sugar plantation to the citizens of Barbados as a means of compensation for his family's participation in the TTA and enslavement of African people in Barbados. These demands followed the revelation that Drax, whose fortune is valued as being at least £150 million, is the wealthiest land-owning member of Parliament, still personally controls the Drax Hall plantation in Barbados. According to historian David Olusoga, "The Drax family are one of the few who were pioneers in the early stages of the British slave economy back in the 17th century and, generations later, still owned plantations and enslaved people at the end of British slavery in the 1830s."[59]

In Jamaica, like the Draxes, the Hibbert family was an affluent family that profited from the benefits of the TTA and enslavement. Following their arrival in Jamaica in the eighteenth century, the Hibbert family was considered among the most successful factors (that is, local speculators who would take large consignments of enslaved people, then sell them to planters across Jamaica for a profit). When enslavers filed claims for compensation in 1834, Thomas Hibbert Jr submitted three claims for 799 enslaved people, totalling £14,337 in compensation. Thomas's cousin George Hibbert also filed claims for 3,453 enslaved people on the nineteen plantations he owned. He received

---

Profits of Slavery", *Yorkshire Post*, 7 May 2019, https://www.yorkshirepost.co.uk/heritage-and-retro/heritage/how-harewood-house-yorkshire-was-built-profits-slavery-1755569.

59. Paul Lashmar and Jonathan Smith, "He's the MP with the Downton Abbey Lifestyle", *Observer*, 12 December 2020, https://www.theguardian.com/world/2020/dec/12/hes-the-mp-with-the-downton-abbey-lifestyle-but-the-shadow-of-slavery-hangs-over-the-gilded-life-of-richard-drax.

£63,050 in compensation, the modern equivalent of £78.40 million.[60]

Wealth generated by the system of slavery has also extended to other present-day institutions, such as trusts. The Dick Bequest in Scotland is one such institution. Established following the death of merchant James Dick, who bequeathed almost £120,000 for educational development in Scotland, the bequest has its origins in the profits from slavery in the Caribbean. In 2021, it was revealed that Dick, after whom the bequest is named, was a trader in the TTA in Kingston, Jamaica. With approximately £1.7 million in the trust at present, calls have been made to return these funds to Jamaica.[61]

## The "Moving Goalpost" Strategy

Each time an argument against reparation is defeated and set aside, a new one is invented and marshalled, and the terms and conditions of the dialogue keep changing. Beckles characterizes this response over time to demands for reparation by the British state as the "moving goalpost strategy". This strategy is best exemplified by former British prime minister David Cameron urging Caribbean people in 2015, during his visit to Jamaica, to "move on from painful legacy" of slavery.

Historian Heather Cateau discerns in statements like Cameron's both an insensitivity (especially coming from one whose ancestors received compensation at the time of Emancipation) and an attempt to mask the experience of the reparation movement as it evolves, in language designed to conceal or reduce its significance. This is where the rhetoric of condemning enslavement but not supporting reparation comes from. That is why former British prime minister Tony Blair could express deep sorrow for enslavement but not apologize for Britain's role in it. Cateau cites and rebuts the following suggestions made by the UK government:

---

60. Ahmed Reid, "History Matters: The Precursor to the Jamaica Chamber of Commerce", *Gleaner*, https://jamaica-gleaner.com/article/focus/20210326/ahmed-reid-history-matters-precursor-jamaica-chamber-commerce.

61. Gabrielle Hemmings, "Reparation: The Greatest Political Tide of Twenty-First Century", *Gleaner*, 9 May 2021, https://jamaica-gleaner.com/article/focus/20210509/reparation-greatest-political-tide-21st-century.

"Instead of reparation we should concentrate on identifying ways forward with a focus on shared global challenges that face our countries in the twenty-first century." (Why not both?)

or:

"We need to increase investment in the region but not directly address reparation."

or:

"We should base our relationship today on the opportunities we can generate together rather than over-relying on the historical ties of the past."

or:

"Britain wants to be your partner in the future, your partner of choice."

Cateau's response to the above statements is to pose this question: "Should these suggestions not fall in line with the goals of the reparation movement and not be part of the counter-argument?"[62]

The Cameron formula of "moving on" for those who benefited from slavery is not a realistic or practical option if the slavery past leaves people and their society in poverty, as it does for the majority of people of the Caribbean. It is a mistake to think of the question of slavery as something that only pertains to its direct victims, past and present. Instead, the response of the British state to the demand for reparation should be to acknowledge slavery's crucial role in helping to establish the present-day system under which ordinary Britons live and labour, connecting them to its enslaving foundations, controlling mechanisms and values. The demand for reparation will have greater support among the British public when they come to realize that, in one respect, they share a common fate with the victimized descendants of enslaved Africans – the persistence of plantation slavery. Plantation slavery may no longer be present in the same form, but its founding principle has never gone away; that is, take as much as you can from the labour of the many and concentrate land and wealth among the few.

---

62. Heather Cateau quoted in Jonathan Guthrie, "Examining the Slave Trade: Britain Has a Debt to Repay", *Financial Times*, 27 June 2020, https://www.ft.com/content/945c6136-0b92-41bf-bd80-a80d944bb0b8.

**Figure 5.1.** Clovis commentary on the *Zong* massacre and reparation

The stance of other complicit European states is not unlike Britain's, but CARICOM states will not be deterred by such negative responses and will continue to press for reparatory justice.

## The #BlackLivesMatter Movement and the European Response

While European countries have continued to stop short of acknowledging the need for reparation, it is important that in the wake of the #BlackLivesMatter movement in the United States and its consequent spread worldwide, key European political and royal figures have made statements acknowledging their roles in slavery and colonialism. In some cases, they have spoken to the need for reparatory justice. Belgium's Princess Marie-Esméralda's public statement condemning its colonial brutality in Congo and demanding reparation is an important one. In an interview conducted in July 2020, Princess Esméralda stated, "It's a difficult conversation for many, especially when we talk about reparation, but it is absolutely necessary if we want to have a just, fair society. So, if we talk about reparation, why not start by fair trade?"[63]

Prior to this, Belgian King Philippe penned a letter of regret for its brutality inflicted in what is now known as the Democratic Republic of Congo to the republic's president. This followed the statement by Belgian prime minister Sophie Wilmès, urging her country to "look its past in the face".[64] With regard to the United Kingdom, British Prince Harry and his wife Meghan Markle publicly stated the following, in reference to the #BlackLivesMatter movement and the protests against historical injustices for people of African descent stemming from slavery and colonialism: "When you look across the Commonwealth, there is no way that we can move forward unless we acknowledge the past."[65]

In addition to this, on 28 May 2021, Germany announced that it would acknowledge the atrocities that it committed against the Nama and Ovaherero people of Namibia in the twentieth century. Under Germany's colonial rule, from 1904 to 1908, tens of thousands of Nama and Ovaherero people were murdered by German colonial forces or expelled to the Omaheke Desert, where many consequently died of starvation and dehydration.

Owing to this, Germany announced its plan to provide financial aid valued at over €1.1 billion, to be paid over the course of thirty years. However, critics, including the Nama and Ovaherero people, have said that this aid is insufficient and that the German government should instead provide a reparation package.[66]

---

63. "Belgian Princess Condemns Her Family's Brutal Colonial History in Congo and Calls for Reparations", *Democracy Now*, 9 July 2020, https://www.democracynow.org/2020/7/9/belgium_colonial_legacy_leopold_ii.

64. Ibid.

65. "Harry and Meghan: 'Wrongs of Past Need to Be Acknowledged', Duke Says", *BBC News*, 6 July 2020, https://www.bbc.com/news/uk-53310896.

66. "Namibian Indigenous People Blast German-Namibian 'Reconciliation Agreement'", *Gleaner*, 20 June 2021, https://jamaica-gleaner.com/article/focus/20210620/namibian-indigenous-people-blast-german-namibian-reconciliation-agreement#slideshow-2.

# 6

# Small Steps, Giant Leaps for Reparation

In 2016, the CRC presented a letter relating to reparatory justice to six heads of European nations – Denmark, France, Portugal, Spain, the Netherlands and the United Kingdom – setting out the basis for the Caribbean reparatory justice movement and the reasons such countries were singled out for claims of redress. Predictably, the response of the British has been to declare that they do not believe reparation is the answer. Spain, for its part, suggested that it had already done enough by contributing to the permanent Memorial to Slavery at the UN headquarters in New York and though the Spanish Agency for International Development Cooperation, which has initiated educational programmes for schools, designed to teach children and young people the history of the Spanish presence in the Americas in both its good and bad aspects. Former French president François Hollande responded that history cannot be erased and that it could not be the subject of transactions at the end of an accounting exercise "which would be, at all points, impossible to establish". This is ironic because Emancipation was made an accounting exercise when the French extracted reparations from Haiti/Ayiti and when the British compensated the enslavers. Of the six recipients of the letter, only Portugal has not responded.

The letter is to be seen as a first practical step in entering a discussion around a development plan. It is about Europeans taking responsibility for what they did to colonized people. European governments have a legal, economic and moral duty to repair the harm done to their former colonies through the extraction of wealth, which left the region underdeveloped.

The CRC has emphasized that reparation is *not* a handout; it is about development – more schools, urban renewal, energy sufficiency, modern agriculture and addressing the crisis in health. European governments and their sympathizers present those arguing for reparation as so-called victims asking for handouts. However, it is not about standing on street corners and asking for handouts or subjecting oneself to any indignity of asking people to give money based on a theory that has emerged out of Europe.[67]

Reparation is to be treated not as an option but as an obligation, and when interpreted in this way there is no substitute for it. Reparation is not *aid* in the sense of the old-fashioned handing out of grants; *aid* is what people of means are required to do to alleviate the burden of those who are less well-off, so *aid* must never be confused with reparation. The wrong done to Caribbean people can never be repaid purely in monetary compensation.

The CRC has been the catalyst in the new thrust for reparation. Emboldened by the support provided by the heads of government of the region since 2013, the CRC has been able to press its claim on the guilty nations of Europe. The work of the CRC is to increasingly legitimize the rightfulness of reparation claims in the eyes of Caribbean nationals, with the aid of solid research through the work of the Centre for the Study of the Legacies of British Slavery at University College London and the Slave Voyages Database at Emory University in the United States, both referenced in chapter 2. In the case of the Slave Voyages Database, its findings in 2018 (the Slave Voyages Database 2.0) provided new information identifying the roles played by countries such as Sweden and Norway and citizens of modern-day Switzerland and Latvia, who were never previously associated with the illegal trade in enslaved Africans and slavery. The database also revealed that at least one ship, the *Goliubchick*,

---

67. Beckles, "Relinquishing Doubt".

flying the Russian flag, made a voyage to Cuba in 1838. This is not an accusation against the Russian state, but evidence of the wide-scale participation of European citizens of many nations in this horrible enterprise, even without the backing of the state per se. The updated database provides additional details related to the activities of countries already identified and allows the CRC to add more countries to the list of those from which it will demand reparation.

## Universities Lead the Way

Several institutions across the years have made earnest steps towards the path of reparation. These have included financial institutions and churches, such as the Southern Baptist Convention, which in 1995 acknowledged and denounced its participation in racism, slavery and segregation, and the Church of England, which in 2006 apologized for the role it played in the eighteenth century in benefiting from the labour of enslaved Africans in the Caribbean. However, the most encouraging sign that combines research and acts of atonement is the increasing number of universities in both the United Kingdom and the United States which have been engaging in research to learn more about their past ties to slavery. In the United Kingdom, the universities of Cambridge, Edinburgh, Oxford and Glasgow all benefited from slavery profits.

## University of Glasgow

The University of Glasgow was the favoured university of enslavers of the Caribbean (especially Jamaica), who sent their sons to Glasgow to study law, medicine and other subjects. As a result, the university received massive endowments from Caribbean enslavers, which enabled it to grow into one of the largest universities in Europe. It is therefore fitting that the University of Glasgow should be the first institution in the United Kingdom to engage in the first clear act of reparation. In a landmark agreement with the University of the West Indies on 31 July 2018, the University of Glasgow committed to establishing the Glasgow–Caribbean Centre for Development Research with funds from that university, with promises of future funding to support the running of the centre, scholarships, research and public engagement. Research will focus on the legacies of slavery and colonialism, revolving around the broad areas and issues of public health – specifically chronic disease, persistent poverty, inequality in economic relations and educational inadequacies. Why is the University of Glasgow's move so significant?

- It represents the first formal response to the Caribbean's call for reparatory justice.
- The provisions fit precisely into elements of the CARICOM Ten-Point Plan.
- The agreement is bound to have a demonstrable effect on other universities and institutions and eventually, governments, particularly the UK government.
- It is an actual example of and proof that reparation has begun.

## Georgetown University

In April 2019, students at Georgetown University in Washington, DC, voted to raise tuition fees to provide reparation to the descendants of 272 enslaved Africans owned and later sold by the school in 1838. The background to this is that when the university was in need of funds, the Jesuit priests who founded and ran the college decided to sell the enslaved on plantations that they owned. The sale resulted in the separation of numerous families and forced hundreds into horrific conditions. That sale at the time raised today's equivalent of US$3.3 million for the university. Earlier, in 2016, the administration of Georgetown University had already decided to give admission preference to the descendants of the enslaved sold by the school. What is significant about Georgetown's actions in 2016 and 2019?

- It undermined the argument of those who oppose reparation on the grounds that the people to whom reparation should be paid are long dead.
- Equally, it gave lie to the argument that even if reparation were to be paid to descendants of enslaved Africans, it would be impossible to identify them.

- The increase in tuition fees was the result of a vote by the student body of Georgetown University, showing a commitment by the current generation to contribute in a practical way to making reparation a reality.

Elsewhere in the United States, Princeton Theological Seminary and Virginia Theological Seminary are the latest institutions to acknowledge and atone for their role in slavery. Princeton Theological Seminary, for its part, has set aside US$25 million to pay reparation for its historical ties to slavery. Specifically naming the announced action as one of reparation, the seminary has pledged itself to telling the truth, even though the institution itself never actually owned enslaved people. However, it benefited from the slave economy through investments in Southern banks and from donors who profited from slavery. Its founding faculty and leaders used enslaved labour during their lifetime and some advocated sending black men and women to Liberia. Payments from the fund created will, among other things, cover thirty new scholarships for students who are descendants of enslaved or from underrepresented groups. Virginia Theological Seminary has also set aside funds totalling US$1.7 million as reparation, after acknowledging that the labour of enslaved African Americans was used on campus, including in the construction of at least one building, the Aspinwall. In addition, the seminary refused to permit the attendance of black students until the 1950s.

These seminaries' acts of reparation are particularly significant for two reasons: first, they strengthen the argument of reparation advocates that there is no statute of limitations on crimes against humanity and, more importantly, that to be guilty, one did not necessarily have to be an owner and exploiter of the enslaved, that the association can be tangential as long as one benefited directly and participated at some level in promoting and maintaining the system. Second, as in the case of the Georgetown University act of reparation, they undermine the defence of the anti-reparation lobby that reparation means cutting cheques and giving handouts to present-day descendants of formerly enslaved, even if their lineage could be traced.

Overall, more than a dozen universities in the United States, including the Ivy League schools Brown University (which has since 2012 established the Center for the Study of Slavery and Justice) and Harvard University, have publicly recognized their ties to slavery. In Canada, Dalhousie University has apologized to the people of African descent in Nova Scotia for its involvement in the TTA and for North American slavery, and it has added a new scholarship for a student of African descent.

## Antigua's Claim against Harvard University's Law School

These actions by US universities inspired Antigua and Barbuda's prime minister Gaston Browne to pen a personal letter, dated 30 October 2019, to the president of Harvard University, in which he pointed out that Harvard's famous law school would not have existed without the labour of his country's people and that the university therefore owed amends to its citizens. The basis for Browne's claim is that over two hundred years ago, a wealthy plantation owner, Isaac Royall Jr, helped to found the Harvard Law School with riches made from slavery. The prime minister's claim coincided with the establishment of a fourth University of the West Indies landed campus in Antigua. Browne was seeking reparation to finance that campus.[68]

A student-generated report released in 2011 had revealed the university's "directly complicit" connection with slavery, and in 2017, the university had hosted a major public conference exploring the long-neglected connections between universities and slavery. During that conference, Daniel Coquillette, co-author of *A History of Harvard Law School*, recounted how the enslaver Royall brutally put down a slave rebellion on Antigua, during which dozens of enslaved people were drawn and quartered or burned at the stake.

It followed claims for reparation on behalf of Antigua and Barbuda by Sir Ronald Sanders, Antiguan ambassador to the United States.

---

68. Adeel Hassan, "Antigua Demands Harvard Pay Reparations for Benefiting from Slavery", *New York Times*, 6 November 2019, https://www.nytimes.com/2019/11/06/us/harvard-antigua-slavery-reparations.html.

While the actions of these universities on both sides of the Atlantic represent small but significant first steps in response to the demands for reparation, the CRC maintains that these institutional responses should not be seen in any way as replacing or diminishing the responsibility of the complicit states to atone and make reparation.

## Other Developments

On 25 May 2020, an African American man, George Floyd, was arrested by police in the state of Minneapolis for, allegedly, making a purchase with a counterfeit US$20 bill. Upon his arrest, white police officer Derek Chauvin pressed his knee into Floyd's neck while he was handcuffed on the ground, for eight minutes and forty-six seconds. Six minutes into Chauvin's assault, Floyd became unresponsive. Though Floyd had repeatedly stated that he could not breathe, other police officers refused to come to his aid. Floyd was then transported to the Hennepin County Medical Center, where he was pronounced dead. This brutal incident, which was caught on camera, came on the heels of the shooting death of an African American woman, Breonna Taylor, on 13 March 2020 by white policemen in her home in Louisville, Kentucky, and the 5 May 2020 release of footage of another African American man, Ahmaud Arbery, being hunted down and killed by two white men in the state of Georgia on 23 February 2020.

These events lit the fire in the resurgence of the #BlackLivesMatter movement, which began in 2013 after a white man was acquitted of murdering Trayvon Martin, an unarmed black teenager.

The resulting protests in 2020 took place not only in the United States but across the globe as people of African descent, and those who stand in solidarity with them, decried white supremacy, historical injustices faced by people of African descent and Afrophobia experienced worldwide. Protests took on many shapes and forms. They have ranged from local protests in the streets or the tearing down of monuments dedicated to white supremacists to professional athletes using their platforms to protest about the injustices faced. This resurgence has also led to renewed calls for reparatory justice. In addition to educational institutions, others such as financial institutions have been forced to confront their involvement in slavery and the TTA, and, as a result, have come forward to apologize for their roles and offer reparatory justice in different forms.

In the United Kingdom, for instance, the pub Greene King has publicly committed to paying reparation for the company's links to and profits from the TTA to the black, Asian and minority ethnic (BAME) community in the United Kingdom after acknowledging that its founder, Benjamin Greene, received compensation after claiming for his "property", that is, enslaved Africans, at Emancipation. In addition to this entity, the insurance institution Lloyd's of London, whose founder subscriber member Simon Fraser received compensation of nearly £400,000 in today's money at Emancipation, has also committed to reparation for BAME groups.[69]

Other institutions have been called out for their links to and profits from slavery and the TTA, including Barclays Bank, the Royal Bank of Scotland, Bank of England and HSBC in the United Kingdom and JP Morgan Chase in the United States.

## Strides in the United States

Prior to this resurgence of the #BlackLivesMatter movement, a small but significant victory for the reparation cause in the United States was achieved on 19 June 2019, when the US House of Representatives judiciary subcommittee met to consider a bill that would create a commission to develop proposals to address the lingering effects of slavery and consider a national apology for the harm it has caused. Symbolically, the hearing was held on Juneteenth, a day commemo-

---

69. Kevin Rawlinson, "Lloyd's of London and Greene King to Make Slave Trade Reparations", *Guardian*, 18 June 2020, https://www.theguardian.com/world/2020/jun/18/lloyds-of-london-and-greene-king-to-make-slave-trade-reparations.

rating the final emancipation of enslaved Africans in the United States (this day officially became a federal holiday in the United States in 2021). The bill dates back to 1989, when Representative John Conyers Jr introduced legislation to create the commission. He was to do so unsuccessfully for thirty years until the 19 June session in 2019, when it was sponsored by Democratic representative Sheila Jackson Lee, from Texas.

The role of the CRC was recognized by the invitation to Sir Hilary Beckles, chairman of the CRC, to be present at the House of Representatives hearing at which Representative Lee acknowledged the Caribbean's leadership role in the global reparation movement. On 14 April 2021, historic progress was made as the House Judiciary Committee voted 25 to 17 to advance the bill to the full House of Representatives for the first time.

While this bill has not had complete success at the federal level yet, the state of California has made its own strides, creating history when Governor Gavin Newsom signed Bill AB 3121 to establish a study and make recommendations in relation to reparation for slavery in September 2020.[70]

Another important development was the establishment of the National African American Reparations Commission in April 2015. The commission is made up of distinguished scholars, experts and activists from across the United States with a "common commitment to fight for reparatory justice, compensation and the restoration of African American communities that were plundered by the historical crimes of slavery, segregation and colonialism and that continue to be victimized by the legacies of slavery and American apartheid".[71] The National African American Reparations Commission has also elaborated a ten-point plan, modelled off that of the CRC.

---

70. Madeline Holcombe, "California Passes a First-of-Its-Kind Law to Consider Reparations for Slavery", *CNN*, 1 October 2020, https://edition.cnn.com/2020/10/01/us/california-bill-slavery-reparations-trnd/index.html.

71. National African American Reparations Commission, https://reparationscomm.org/about-naarc/. The website also contains an extensive collection of reparation-related content, including news, commentaries, lectures, conferences and seminars.

The reparation movement in the United States faces similar challenges to those being encountered by the movement in the Caribbean. As in the case of the CARICOM Ten-Point Plan, advocates in the United States have been at pains to emphasize that reparation does not necessarily mean that the federal government would be writing cheques to black people. Rather, the federal government could offer various types of assistance – such as zero-interest loans for prospective black homeowners, free university tuition, community development plans to spur growth of black-owned businesses in black neighbourhoods – to address the social and economic fallout from slavery and racially discriminatory policies that have resulted in a huge wealth gap between black and white people.

### Opposition to the Idea of Reparation

Despite these clear signs of progress and overt acts of reparation by institutions and countries associated with the TTA and slavery, there remains within the Caribbean, the United States, and no doubt in Africa, scepticism among black people, who see the campaign for reparation as either impractical, with no chance of success, or a forlorn hope among dreamers. This doubt is best exemplified by a column in the Jamaica *Gleaner,* in which the writer declares reparation to be "a project of misguided political and intellectual elites" and further describes it as "a strategy to shift blame from politicians and their counterparts to the British for the prominence of their ancestors in slavery".[72] A 2019 research poll, conducted by the Associated Press–NORC Center for Public Affairs Research in the United States, found that most Americans oppose reparation for slavery. However, there was a large divide between Americans of different racial and ethnic backgrounds, with 74 per cent of black people in favour of reparation, compared to 15 per cent of white Americans. Among Hispanics, the poll found that 44 per cent favoured reparation.

---

72. Lipton Matthews, "Slavery Is a Scapegoat for the Failures of the Political and Intellectual Classes", *Gleaner,* 21 October 2019, http://jamaica-gleaner.com/article/commentary/20191021/lipton-matthews-slavery-scapegoat-failures-political-and-intellectual.

Beckles addressed the question of doubt in delivering the second Sister Mary Noelle Menezes Lecture in Georgetown, Guyana, on 25 January 2019,[73] when he compared doubt about freedom a few years before Emancipation with doubt today about the feasibility of reparation: "How do we go beyond doubt; how do we imagine a future and how do we do what seems impossible?" The answer may well lie in approaching the issue from a historical perspective. Few of our enslaved ancestors could have imagined the possibility of Emancipation in 1838 after four hundred years of enslavement, and yet it happened, so it is not surprising that few black people would believe that reparation could ever happen, but it *is* happening.

## On the Other Hand

In an article published in the *Washington Post* (31 January 2020), Thai Jones argues that policies like the one described at Georgetown University suggest a specific set of conditions that could lead to action: an institution culpable in the past and still in existence; a discrete and identifiable population able to show that they or their ancestors suffered harm from enslavement; and a community to fight on the claimants' behalf.[74] As a strategy in the fight for reparation, a local focus, whether institutional (like a university or a church denomination) or a large corporation, means that activists have more immediate access to institutional pressure points. Decision-makers are also often less shielded from criticism and thus more likely to yield.

## National Action Still the Object

However, as important and significant as these concessions are, none of those policies can replace national action. Nor can individual

---

73. "The Second Distinguished Lecture: Sr Mary Noel Menezes, by Professor Sir Hilary Beckles", University of Guyana, https://fb.watch/6iopaQouyh/.
74. Thai Jones, "Slavery Reparations Seem Impossible. In Many Places They Are Already Happening", *Washington Post*, 31 January 2020, https://www.washingtonpost.com/outlook/2020/01/31/slavery-reparations-seem-impossible-many-places-theyre-already-happening/.

expressions of remorse stand in for a formal apology on behalf of the enslaved and their descendants. "A systematic crime requires a systematic response. No partial undertaking can substitute for such a step."⁷⁵

## Conclusion

Bert Samuels, a member of the Jamaica National Council on Reparation, boldly declares that the movement is here to stay. "Our freedom was not a one-day, one-week or one-century battle. It was won with the collective effort and sacrifice of Tacky, Sam Sharpe, Nanny and countless fighters for freedom and justice."⁷⁶ And Beckles:

> It took all of the nineteenth century to eradicate slavery from the modern world, one hundred years from the beginning, with the Haitians in 1804 abolishing slavery forever and ever to 1888 in Brazil. It took one hundred years to uproot it and get it out of our moral world. . . . Then the twentieth century – another one hundred years to get rid of indentureship, to get the right to vote, the right to have trade unions, to educate our children, the civil rights movement, independence; it took all of the twentieth century to get those fundamental civil and human rights. And now we have a long twenty-first century in front of us and I am saying to you that the greatest movement in the world in the twenty-first century is going to be the reparation movement.⁷⁷

Students of Caribbean history, whether at the school or university level, live in an exciting time when they can experience history in the making. Whereas the study of emancipation in the Caribbean, the civil rights movement in the United States, the struggle against

---

75. Ibid.
76. Bert Samuels, "#reparationNOW!", *Jamaica Observer,* 28 October 2019, https://www.jamaicaobserver.com/opinion/-reparationnow-a-call-for-support_178039.
77. Hilary Beckles, "Historical Realities for Redress: The Adequacy of Relinquishing Reservations and Pursuing Reparations" (Sister Mary Noel Menezes Distinguished Lecture, Georgetown, Guyana, 25 January 2019), https://fb.watch/6iopaQouyh/.

apartheid in South Africa, and the anti-colonial and independence movement in Barbados, or Jamaica or Guyana are done from hindsight as recorded historical events, the reparation movement, which represents yet another stage in the fight for social justice for black people, is a live and living activity. It presents an opportunity to study events along an interconnected, unbroken continuum from life in precolonial Africa, the Caribbean and the Americas to the yet-unfinished struggle for reparatory justice that is in itself a lesson of history unfolding and affecting the present.

Reparation is a just cause. In the words of US activist Lawrence Hamm (quoting the slogan of the December 12th Movement), "They stole us, they sold us, they owe us!"[78] Sir Ellis Clarke, who was the Trinidad and Tobago government's UN representative to a subcommittee of the Committee on Colonialism in 1964, agrees:

> An administering power . . . is not entitled to extract for centuries all that can be got out of a colony and when that has been done to relieve itself of its obligations by the conferment of a formal but meaningless – meaningless because it cannot possibly be supported – political independence. Justice requires that reparation be made to the country that has suffered the ravages of colonialism before that country is expected to face up to the problems and difficulties that will inevitably beset it upon independence.

Anything less than that, Clarke concluded, "would constitute something less than the genuine article; it would be trying to fob off West Indians with independence on the cheap".[79]

---

78. Stephen Milles, "They Stole Us, They Sold Us, They Owe Us!", *Workers World*, 28 June 2018, https://www.workers.org/2018/06/37960/. See also the December 12th Movemement, http://d12m.com/.

79. Quoted in Gordon K. Lewis, *The Growth of the Modern West Indies* (New York: Monthly Review Press, 1968), 385.

# Appendix

Select Compensation Claims for the Caribbean (Male), Ranked from Highest to Lowest, Showing Modern-Day Equivalencies

| Name | Number of Claims | Enslaved Claimed | Compensation | Modern Equivalent (in £m) |
|---|---|---|---|---|
| George Rainy | 30 | 2,585 | 145,695 | 181.1 |
| Charles McGarel | 14 | 2,827 | 135,076 | 168.0 |
| Charles Stewart Parker | 16 | 2,176 | 114,663 | 143.0 |
| John Gladstone | 11 | 2,912 | 112.716 | 140.1 |
| Rowland Mitchell | 30 | – | 98,944 | 123.0 |
| James Patrick McInroy | 9 | 1,741 | 91,334 | 114.0 |
| James Blair | 1 | 1,598 | 83,530 | 104.0 |
| Andrew Colvile | 19 | 3,647 | 70,786 | 88.0 |
| Charles Porcher Lang | 9 | 1,438 | 66,605 | 83.0 |
| George Hibbert | 19 | 3,453 | 63,050 | 78.4 |
| **Total** | **158** | **15,277** | **869,796** | **1,081.0** |

*Source:* Centre for the Study of the Legacies of British Slavery, University College London, www.ucl.ac.uk/lbs; calculations taken from https://www.measuringworth.com/ppoweruk/.

# Selected Bibliography

## Books and Articles

Beckles, Hilary McD. *Britain's Black Debt: Reparations for Caribbean Slavery and Native Genocide*. Kingston: University of the West Indies Press, 2013.

———. "The Reparation Movement: Greatest Political Tide of the Twenty-First Century". *Social and Economic Studies* 68, nos. 3–4 (2019): 9–26.

———. "White Labour in Black Slave Plantation Society and Economy: A Case Study of Indentured Labour in Seventeenth Century Barbados". PhD dissertation, University of Hull, 1980.

Beckles, Hilary McD., and Verene A. Shepherd. *Liberties Lost: The Indigenous Caribbean and Slave Systems*. Cambridge: Cambridge University Press, 2004.

———. *Saving Souls: The Struggle to End the Transatlantic Trade in Africans*. Kingston: Ian Randle, 2007.

———. *Trading Souls: Europe's Transatlantic Trade in Africans*. Kingston: Ian Randle, 2007.

Burnard, Trevor. *Mastery, Tyranny and Desire: Thomas Thistlewood and His Slaves in the Anglo-Jamaican World*. Chapel Hill: University of North Carolina Press; Kingston: University of the West Indies Press, 2004.

Coates, Ta-Nehisi. "The Case for Reparations". *Atlantic*, June 2014. https://www.theatlantic.com/magazine/archive/2014/06/the-case-for-reparations/361631/.

Comissiong, David. "The Reparations Manifesto". Institute of the Black World 21st Century, 13 December 2017. https://ibw21.org/reparations/the-reparations-manifesto/.

DeGruy, Joy, "Post-Traumatic Slave Syndrome". Part 2. Black Bag Speakers Series, Portland State University, 17 October 2006. YouTube video, https://www.youtube.com/watch?v=lNAtEXavTF4.

Drayton, Richard. "Slavery and the City of London". Gresham College, 28 October 2019. https://s3-eu-west-1.amazonaws.com/content.gresham.ac.uk/data/binary/3137/2019-10-28_RichardDrayton_SlaveryCity-T.pdf.

Dick, Devon "God Has Done Us an Injustice: A Baptist Pastor Makes a Biblical Case for Reparations". *Jamaica Global*, 26 July 2019. https://www.jamaicaglobalonline.com/god-has-done-us-an-injustice-a-baptist-pastor-makes-a-biblical-case-for-reparations/.

Equiano, Olaudah. *The Interesting Narrative of the Life of Olaudah Equiano, or Gustavus Vass*. 1789. Available at https://www.gutenberg.org/files/15399/15399-h/15399-h.htm.

Gifford, Anthony. "Key Legal Aspects of the Claim for Reparation". *Social and Economic Studies* 68, nos. 3–4 (2019): 230–32.

———. "The Legal Basis of the Claim for Slavery Reparation", *Human Rights Magazine* 27, 2 (2000). https://www.americanbar.org/groups/crsj/publications/human_rights_magazine_home/human_rights_vol27_2000/spring2000/hr_spring00_gifford/.

———. *The Passionate Advocate*. Kingston: Arawak, 2007.

Hall, Douglas. *In Miserable Slavery: Thomas Thistlewood in Jamaica, 1750–86*. Kingston: University of the West Indies Press, 1999.

Hira, Sandew. *20 Questions and Answers about Reparations for Colonialism*. The Hague: Amrit, 2014.

IBW21. "Marcus Garvey on Reparations". Institute of the Black World 21st Century, 4 August 2017. https://ibw21.org/reparations/marcus-garvey-reparations/.

Keegan, William F., and Corinne L. Hofman. *The Caribbean before Columbus*. Oxford: Oxford University Press, 2017.

Lewis, W. Arthur. *Labour in the West Indies: The Birth of a Workers' Movement*. 1939. Reprint, London: New Beacon, 1977.

Mbeki, G. *The Struggle for Liberation in South Africa*. Cape Town: University of the Western Cape, 1992.

Newton, Grace, "How Harewood House in Yorkshire Was Built with Profits of Slavery". *Yorkshire Post*, 7 May 2019. https://www.yorkshirepost.co.uk/heritage-and-retro/heritage/how-harewood-house-yorkshire-was-built-profits-slavery-1755569.

Palmer, Colin A. *Eric Williams and the Making of the Modern Caribbean*. Chapel Hill: University of North Carolina Press, 2006.

Patterson, Orlando. *The Sociology of Slavery: An Analysis of the Origins,*

*Development, and Structure of Negro Slave Society in Jamaica*. London: McGibbon and Kee, 1967.

Prince, Mary. *The History of Mary Prince, a West Indian Slave, Related by Herself*, edited by Moira Ferguson. 1831. London: Pandora, 1987.

Robinson, Randall. *The Debt: What America Owes to Blacks*. New York: Penguin, 2001.

Shepherd, Verene. "Caribbean Women and Reparatory Justice". *Gleaner*, 7 March 2021. https://jamaica-gleaner.com/article/focus/20210307/verene-shepherd-caribbean-women-and-reparatory-justice.

———. *Maharani's Misery: Narratives of a Passage from India to the Caribbean*. Kingston: University of the West Indies Press, 2002.

Shepherd, Verene A., and Hilary McD. Beckles, eds. *Caribbean Slavery in the Atlantic World: A Student Reader*. Kingston: Ian Randle, 2000.

Shepherd, Verene A., and Ahmed Reid. "Women, Slavery and the Reparation Movement in the Caribbean". *Social and Economic Studies* 68, nos. 3–4 (2019): 27–53.

Shepherd, Verene, Ahmed Reid, Cavell Francis and Kameika Murphy, eds. *Jamaica and the Debate over Reparation for Slavery: A Discussion Paper*. Prepared by the Jamaica National Bicentenary Committee. Kingston: Pelican, 2012.

Small, Stephen, and Sandew Hira. *20 Questions and Answers about Dutch Slavery and Its Legacy*. The Hague: Amrit, 2014.

*Social and Economic Studies*, special issue on reparations, 68, nos. 3–4 (2019).

Walvin, James. *The Zong: A Massacre, the Law and the End of Slavery*. New Haven: Yale University Press, 2011.

Wedderburn, Robert. *The Horrors of Slavery and other Writings by Robert Wedderburn*, edited by Iain McCalman. Princeton, NJ: Markus Wiener, 1991.

Wilson, Richard A. *The Politics of Truth and Reconciliation in South Africa: Legitimizing the Post-Apartheid State*. Cambridge: Cambridge University Press, 2001.

Zunder, Armand. "A New Look on the Economic History of Suriname: Including a Methodology to Calculate Reparations for Damage Caused by Dutch Colonial Rule". *Academic Journal of Suriname* 2 (2011): 150–67. http://www.adekusjournal.sr/adekusjournal/data/documentbestand/Artikel_Zunder_def.pdf?sessionid=84?.

## Websites

CARICOM Reparations Commission. https://caricomreparations.org/.
Center for the Study of Slavery, Brown University. https://cssj.brown.edu/.
Centre for the Study of the Legacies of British Slavery, University College London. https://www.ucl.ac.uk/lbs.
International Network of Scholars and Activists for Afrikan Reparations, University of Edinburgh. https://www.inosaar.llc.ed.ac.uk/.
Lowcountry Digital History Initiative. https://ldhi.library.cofc.edu/.
National African-American Reparations Commission. https://reparationscomm.org/.
Understanding Slavery Initiative. http://understandingslavery.com/.
Voyages: The Trans-Atlantic Slave Trade Database. https://www.slavevoyages.org.

www.ingramcontent.com/pod-product-compliance
Lightning Source LLC
Chambersburg PA
CBHW031600170426
43196CB00031B/420